Portraits
REAL AND IMAGINARY

ERNEST BOYD

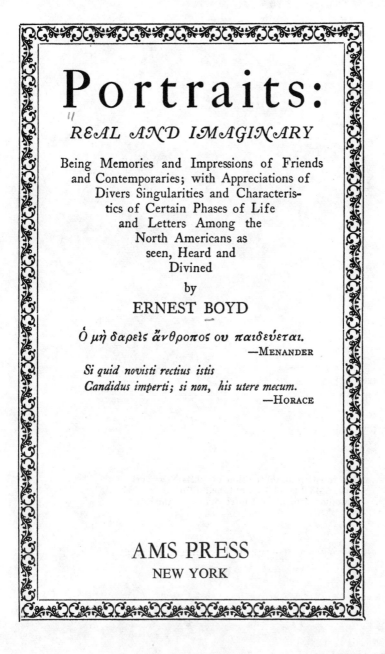

Portraits:

REAL AND IMAGINARY

Being Memories and Impressions of Friends
and Contemporaries; with Appreciations of
Divers Singularities and Characteristics of Certain Phases of Life
and Letters Among the
North Americans as
seen, Heard and
Divined

by

ERNEST BOYD

Ὁ μὴ δαρεὶς ἄνθροπος ου παιδεύεται.
—MENANDER

Si quid novisti rectius istis
Candidus imperti; si non, his utere mecum.
—HORACE

AMS PRESS
NEW YORK

Reprinted from the edition of 1924, New York
First AMS EDITION published 1970
Manufactured in the United States of America

International Standard Book Number: 0-404-00965-4

Library of Congress Catalog Card Number: 77-126702

AMS PRESS, INC.
NEW YORK, N.Y. 10003

For

CONSTANCE and HARRY C. BLACK,
like these,
My friends from both sides
of the Atlantic

Contents

IMAGINARY

Reconstructions

REAL

Impressions

viii   Contents

IMAGINARY

Reconstructions

1. ÆSTHETE: MODEL 1924

HE is a child of this Twentieth Century, for the Yellow Nineties had flickered out in the delirium of the Spanish-American War when his first gurgles rejoiced the ears of his expectant parents. If Musset were more than a name to him, a hazy recollection of French literature courses, he might adapt a line from the author of *La Confession d'un Enfant du Siècle* and declare: I came too soon into a world too old. But no such doubts trouble his spirit, for he believes that this century is his because he was born with it. He does not care who makes its laws, so long as he makes its literature. To this important task he has consecrated at least three whole years of his conscious —or rather self-conscious—existence, and nothing, as yet, has happened to shake his faith in his star. In fact, he finds the business rather easier than he anticipated when, in the twilight sleep of the classroom, vague reports reached him of Milton's infinitesimal fee for "Paradise Lost," of Chatterton's death, of the harassed lives of Shelley and Keats, of the eternal struggle of the artist against the indifference of his age and the foul bludgeonings of fate.

The Æsthete's lot has been a happier one. His thirtieth birthday is still on the horizon, his literary

11

baggage is small or non-existent—but he is already famous; at least, so it seems to him when he gazes upon his own reflection in the eyes of his friends and fingers aggressively the luxurious pages of the magazine of which he is Editor-in-Chief, Editor, Managing Editor, Associate Editor, Contributing Editor, Bibliographical Editor, or Source Material Editor. His relationship to the press must always be editorial, and to meet the changed conditions of the cosmos, a changed conception of the functions of an editor provides him with a vast selection of titles from which to choose. The essential fact is that he has an accredited mouthpiece, a letterhead conferring authority, a secure place from which to bestride the narrow world in which he is already a colossus. Thus he is saved from those sordid encounters with the harsh facts of literary commerce which his predecessors accepted as part of the discipline of life: Meredith reading manuscripts for Chapman and Hall, Gissing toiling in New Grub Street, Anatole France writing prefaces for Lemerre's classics, Dreiser polishing dime novels for Street and Smith.

It is natural that he should thus be overpowered by a mere sense of his own identity, for there is nothing, alas, in his actual achievements, past or present, to warrant his speaking prematurely with the voice of authority. That he does so unchallenged is a proof to him that he himself is his own excuse for being. In a very special sense he accepts the Cartesian formula: I think, therefore I am. When he went to Harvard—or was it Princeton or Yale?—in the early years of the Woodrovian epoch, he was just one of so many mute and inglorious Babbitts preparing to qualify as regular fellows. If some brachycephalic shadow lay across the Nordic blondness of his social pretensions, then, of course, the pilgrimage assumed something of the character of a great adventure into the Promised Land, the penetration to an Anglo-Saxon Lhassa. His immediate concern, in any case, was to resemble as closely as possible every man about him, to acquire at once the marks of what is known as the education of a gentleman, to wit, complete and absolute conformity to conventions, the suppression of even the faintest stirrings of eccentric personality. To this day he feels a little embarrassed when he calls on his father in Wall Street, carrying a walking-stick and wearing a light tweed suit, but he trusts that even the door-opener's scorn will be softened by the knowledge that here is an artist whose personality must be untrammeled.

Those who knew the Æsthete during the period of his initiation will recall how he walked along the banks of his Yankee Isis, or lolled behind the bushes, discussing Life; how he stood at the Leif Ericson monument and became aware of the passage of time;—*Eheu fugaces, labunter anni*, he now would say, especially if he were writing a notice of the Music Box Review; how he went to the cemetery to contemplate the graves of William and Henry James, and noted in himself the incipient thrill of Harvard pride and acquired New Englandism. But these gentle pursuits did not mean so much to him at first as the more red-blooded diversions of week-ends in Boston, and such other fleshly sins as that decayed city might with impunity offer. More refined were the evening parties on the northern side of the town where, in a background of red plush curtains and chairs but recently robbed of their prudish antimacassars, whispers of romantic love might be heard from well-behaved young women, whose highest destiny, before lapsing legally into the arms of a professor, was to be remembered when, at a later stage, a sonnet evolved from a brain beginning to teem creatively. For the rest, football, games and lectures, the former seriously, the latter intermittently, maintained in him the consciousness of the true purpose of a university education.

From the excellent Professors Copeland and Kittredge he distractedly and reluctantly acquired a knowledge of the elements of English composition and of the more virtuous facts of English literature. He read, that is to say, fragments of the classical authors and dutifully absorbed the opinions of academic commentators upon them. American literature was revealed to him as a pale and obedient provincial cousin, whose past contained occasional indiscretions, such as Poe and Whitman, about whom the less said the better. Latin and French were filtered through the same kind of sieve, but without so many precautions, for in neither case was it possible for the aspirant after knowledge to decipher easily the kind of author to whom the urge of adolescence would naturally drive him. The Loeb classics left the un-Christian passages in the original, while the estimable Bohn unkindly took refuge in Italian, the language of a "lust-ridden country, as Anthony Comstock points out in that charming book of his, "Traps for the Young." However, he still possesses enough Latin to be able to introduce into his written discourse appropriate tags from the Dictionary of Classical Quotations, though his quantities, I regret to say, are very weak. I have heard him stress the wrong syllable when speaking of Ouspensky's *Tertium Organum*, although he will emend a corrupt passage in Petronius, and profess to have read all the obscurer authors in Gourmont's *Latin Mystique*.

There came finally a subtle change in his outlook, from which one must date the actual birth of the Æsthete as such—*der Æsthetiker an sich*, so to speak. I suspect it was after one of those parties in the red plush drawing-rooms, when he returned to his rooms with what seemed like the authentic beginnings of a sonnet in his ears. From that moment he had a decided list in the direction of what he called "creative work." While the stadium shook with the hoarse shouts of the rabble at football games he might be observed going off with a companion to indulge in the subtle delights of intellectual conversation. His new friends were those whom he had at first dismissed as negligible owing to their avowed intention of not being he-men. The pulsation of new life within him prompted him to turn a more sympathetic eye upon this hitherto despised set, and they, in their turn, welcomed a new recruit, for the herd instinct is powerful even amongst the intellectual. Under this new guidance he came into contact with ideas undreamt of in the simple philosophy of the classroom. Strange names were bandied about, curious magazines, unwelcomed by the college library, were read, and he was only too glad to discover that all the literary past of which he was ignorant or strangely misinformed counted as nothing in the eyes of his newly emancipated friends. From the pages of the "Masses" he gathered that the Social Revolution was imminent, that Brieux was a dramatist of ideas; in the "Little Review" he was first to learn the enchantment of distance as he sat bemused by its specimens of French and pseudo-French literature. Thus the ballast of which he had to get rid in order to float in the rarefied atmosphere of Advanced Thought was negligible. He had merely to exchange one set of inaccurate ideas for another.

It was at this precise moment in his career that the Wilsonian storming of Valhalla began. With the call to arms tingling in his blood, the Æsthete laid aside the adornments of life for the stern realities of a military training camp. Ancestral voices murmured in his ears, transmitted by instruments of dubious dolichocephalism, it is true, but perhaps all the more effective on that account, for Deep calls unto Deep. I will not dwell upon the raptures of that martial period, for he himself has left us his retrospective and disillusioned record of it, which makes it impossible to recapture the original emotion. Harold Cabot Lilienthal—and, I suppose I should add, in deference to my subject, *hoc genus omne*—was apparently not capable of the strain of ingesting the official facts about the great moral crusade. It was government contract material and proved to be as shoddy and unreliable as anything supplied by the dollar-a-year men to the War Department. By the time the uniformed Æsthete got to France he was a prey to grave misgivings, and as his subsequent prose and verse show, he was one of C. E. Montague's Disenchanted—he who had been a Fiery Particle. He bitterly regretted the collegiate patriotism responsible for his devotion to the lofty rhetoric of the "New Republic." By luck or cunning, however, he succeeded in getting out of the actual trenches, and there, in the hectic back-wash of war, he cultivated the tender seeds just beginning to germinate. He edited his first paper, the "Doughboys' Dreadnought," or under the auspices of the propaganda and vaudeville department made his first contribution to literature, "Young America and Yougo-Slavia." Simultaneously with this plunge into arms and letters he made his first venture into the refinements of sex, thereby extending his French vocabulary and gaining that deep insight into the intimate life of France which is still his proudest possession.

When militarism was finally overthrown, democracy made safe, and a permanent peace established by the victorious and united Allies, he was ready to stay on a little longer in Paris, and to participate in the joys of La Rotonde and Les Deux Magots. There for a brief spell he breathed the same air as the Dadaists, met Picasso and Philippe Soupault, and allowed Ezra Pound to convince him that the French nation was aware of the existence of Jean Cocteau, Paul Morand, Jean Giraudoux and Louis Aragon. From those who had nothing to say on the subject when Marcel Proust published *Du Côté de chez Swann* in 1913 he now learned what a great author the man was, and formed those friendships which caused him eventually to join in a tribute to Proust by a group of English admirers who would have stoned Oscar Wilde had they been old enough to do so when it was the right thing to do.

The time was now ripe for his repatriation, and so, with the same critical equipment in French as in English, but with a still imperfect control of the language as a complication, the now complete Æsthete returned to New York and descended upon Greenwich Village. His poems of disenchantment were in the press, his war novel was nearly finished, and it was not long before he appeared as Editor-in-Chief, Editor, Managing Editor, Associate Editor, Contributing Editor, Assistant Editor, Bibliographical Editor or Source Material Editor of one of the little reviews making no compromise with the public (or any other) taste. Both his prose and verse were remarkable chiefly for typographical and syntactical eccentricities, and a high pressure of un-idiomatic, misprinted French to the square inch. His further contributions (if any) to the art of prose narrative have consisted of a breathless phallic symbolism—a sex obsession which sees the curves of a woman's body in every object not actually flat, including, I need hardly say, the Earth, our great Mother.

But it is essentially as an appraiser of the arts, as editor and critic, that the young Æsthete demands attention. He writes a competent book review and awakes to find himself famous. The next number of the magazine contains a study of his æsthetic, preferably by the author whose work he has favorably reviewed. By the end of the year a publisher announces a biographical and critical study of our young friend, and his fame is assured. He can now discourse with impunity about anything, and he avails himself of the opportunity. He has evolved an ingenious style, florid, pedantic,

technical, full of phrases so incomprehensible or so
rhetorical that they almost persuade the reader that
they must have a meaning. But the skeptical soon
discover that this is an adjustable and protean
vocabulary, that by a process of reshuffling the same
phrases will serve for an artistic appreciation of
Charlie Chaplin, an essay on Marcel Proust, or an
article on Erik Satie. His other expedient is an
arid and inconceivable learning, picked up at second
hand. Let him discuss "The Waste Land" and his
erudition will rival the ponderous fatuity of T. S.
Eliot himself. He will point out on Ptolemy's map
the exact scene, quote the more obscure hymns of
Hesiod, cite an appropriate passage from Strabo's
geography, and conclude with a cryptic remark from
the Fourth Ennead of Plotinus. Yet, one somehow
suspects that even the parasangs of the first chapter
of Xenophon's "Anabasis" would strain his Greek
to the breaking point.

Nevertheless, information is the one thing the
Æsthete dreads. To be in the possession of solid
knowledge and well-digested facts, to have definite
standards, background and experience, is to place
oneself outside the pale of true æstheticism. While
foreign literature is his constant preoccupation, the
Æsthete has no desire to make it known. What
he wants to do is to lead a cult, to communicate
a mystic faith in his idols, rather than to make
them available for general appreciation. Articles
on the subject are an important feature of his magazine, but they consist, as a rule, of esoteric witticisms and allusive gossip about fourth-rate people
whom the writer happens to have met in a café.
He will sweep aside the finest writers in French

as lumber, launch into ecstasies over some Dadaist,
and head the article with a French phrase which
is grammatically incorrect and entirely superfluous,
since it expresses no idea that could not be correctly
rendered in English. If one protest that the very
title of a book which is a masterpiece of style has
been mistranslated, that the first page has several
gross errors, the Æsthete will blandly point out that
in paragraph two there are four abstract nouns each
with a different termination. It is useless to show
him that there are no equivalent nouns in the text.
Finally one gives up arguing, for one remembers
that Rimbaud once wrote a poem about the color
of the vowels.

The almost Swedenborgian mysticism of the
Æsthete is implied in all his comments, for he is
usually inarticulate and incomprehensible. He will
ingenuously describe himself as being "with no more
warning than our great imagination in the presence
of a masterpiece." One reads on to discover the
basis for this enthusiasm, but at the outset one is
halted by the naïve admonition that "it isn't even
important to know that I am right in my judgment.
The significant and to me overwhelming thing was
that the work was a masterpiece and altogether
contemporary." In other words, this work, which
the writer says "I shall make no effort to describe,"
may or may not be a masterpiece, nevertheless it is
one . . . presumably because it is "altogether contemporary." It is on this point of view that the
solemn service of the Younger Æstheticism depends.
If a piece of sculpture is distorted and hideous, if
the battered remains of a wrecked taxi are labeled,
"La Ville Tentaculaire," the correct attitude is one

of delight. One should "make no effort to describe" what is visible, but clutch at the "altogether contemporaneous" element, indicating a masterpiece. In music one must not seek in the cacophonies of the current idols the gross, bourgeois emotion which one receives from Brahms and Beethoven. The Æsthete holds that a *cliché*, in French for preference, will dispose of any genius. One should make play with *le côté Puccini* and *le faux bon*.

The pastime is an amusing one, for it involves no more serious opposition than is to be found in the equally limited arsenal of the Philistines. What could be easier than to caper in front of the outraged mandarins waving volumes of eccentrically printed French poetry and conspuing the gods of the bourgeoisie? It is like mocking a blind man, who hears the insults but cannot see the gestures. The Æsthete tries to monopolize the field of contemporary foreign art, and he is accustomed to respectful submission or the abuse and indifference of sheer ignorance. When he needs a more responsive victim he turns his attention to the arts adored by the crowd, the "lively arts," Mr. Seldes calls them, as if the Fifth Symphony were depressing. The esoteric reviews publish "stills" of Goldwyn pictures and discover strange beauties in follow-up letters and street-car advertisements. The knees of Ann Pennington, the clowning of Charlie Chaplin, the humors of Joe Cook and Fannie Brice must now be bathed in the vapors of æsthetic mysticism. But here there is a difference. The performances of the "lively" artist are familiar to every one above the age of ten; most of us have enjoyed them without feeling compelled to explain ourselves. A reference to Gaby Deslys finds its place as naturally in the works of Havelock Ellis as one to "Der Untergang des Abendlandes." But the Æsthete takes his lively arts uneasily. He is determined to demonstrate that he is just as other men. It is evidently not only in foreigners that one encounters that "certain condescension" of which the late Mr. Lowell complained.

In the last analysis the Æsthete may be diagnosed as the literary counterpart of the traditional American tourist in Paris. He is glamored by the gaudy spectacle of that most provincial of all great cities. French is the tube through which he is fed, and he has not yet discovered how feeble the nourishment is. When he turns to other countries, Germany, for instance, he betrays himself by an incongruous and belated enthusiasm for the novelties of the eighties and nineties. The contemporaries of Thomas Mann, Schnitzler and Hauptmann elsewhere are beneath his notice. Spain and Italy come onto his horizon only when Paris becomes aware of their existence. In a few years, however, his younger brother will go up to Cambridge, in his turn, and then we shall doubtless be enlightened concerning the significant form of Kasimir Edschmid, Walter von Molo and Carl Sternheim. One cannot be "altogether contemporary" all the time.

The signs, indeed, already point that way, for I notice that Hugo Stinnes is mentioned as a modern Marco Polo, and the American realtor is praised as a reincarnation of the creative will of Leonardo da Vinci. This new-found delight in publicity experts, election slogans, billboards and machinery may result in a pilgrimage across the Rhine, where, in the dissolution of so many fine things, an æsthetic of Philistinism has emerged. The tone of democratic yearning which has begun to permeate German literature, recalling the dreams of Radical England in the days of Lord Morley's youth, may facilitate the understanding between two great democracies. But the fatal attraction of French, not to mention the difficulty of German, is a serious obstacle to any new orientation of the younger Æstheticism, and Paris, as usual, can provide what its customers demand. Thus the cult of the movies, with its profound meditations on "Motion Picture Dynamics," and all the vague echoes of Elie Faure's theory of "cineplastics," involves a condemnation of "The Cabinet of Dr. Caligari," a tactless Teuton effort to put some genuine fantasy into the cinema. Instead of that the faithful are called upon by a French expert to admire the films of William S. Hart and Jack Pickford, and some one carefully translates the poetic rhapsodies inspired in him by the contemplation of their masterpieces.

"Two souls," in the words of the German bard, "dwell in the breast" of the Æsthete, and his allegiance is torn between the sales manager's desk, where, it appears, the Renaissance artist of to-day is to be found, and the esoteric editorial chair where experiments are made with stories which "discard the old binding of plot and narrative," the substitute being "the structural framework which appeals to us over and above the message of the line." Thus it becomes possible simultaneously to compare Gertrude Stein with Milton and to chant the glories of the machine age in America. This dualism, ob-

viously, foreshadows the ultimate disintegration of
the type, although for the moment the process is
ingeniously disguised by such devices as the printing
of prose bearing all the outward marks of super-
modern eccentricity but made up cunningly of a pat-
tern woven from phrases culled from billboards and
the advertising pages of the magazines; by repro-
ducing the weirdest pictures together with business-
like photographs of cash registers and telephones.
The household gods of Babbitt are being pressed
into service, just as his innocent amusements are
being intellectualized.

Here the Æsthete departs from the traditions of
the species at his peril. Hitherto his technique has
been perfect, for it has been his practice to confine
his enthusiasm to works of art that are either as
obscure or as inessential, or both, as his own critical
comment. He realized that it was unsafe to trifle
with subjects about which his public might be better
informed than himself. Now his incantations lose
their potency when applied to matters within the
experience and comprehension of the plain people,
and one cubit is added to the stature of William S.
Hart, so far as his devotees are concerned, by the
knowledge that his name is pronounced with æsthetic
reverence on the Left Bank of the Seine.

The process of change is at work, for the transi-
tional youth is already in at least one editorial chair,
frowning upon the frivolities of the Jazz Age, calling for brighter and better books, his dreams haunted
by fears of Sodom and Gomorrah. The Æsthete,
meanwhile, is retiring with an intellectual *Katzenjammer*, which produces in some cases a violent and
unnatural nausea, a revulsion against the wild de-

lights of his former debauches. In others the result is a return to the cozy hearth of the American family; his head aches a little, but his hand is steady. He is refreshed by a journalistic bromo seltzer. There is pep in the swing of his fist upon the typewriter as he sits down to a regular and well-paid job, convincing others, as his employer has convinced him, that he really knows what the public wants.

2. A LITERARY LADY

AGE often withers, but custom never stales her infinite variety. She is with us in all her phases and adds not a little to the culpable, as well as the innocent, merriment of literary life. When one first beholds her she is usually young and eager; her final incarnation is a portly self-sufficiency or an acidulous dissatisfaction. If she were a man she would be either a Falstaff or an Ignatius Loyola, for a fleshly geniality or a spare intensity is the end of all flesh that clothes the ardent soul of the literary lady. Fortunately, when she reaches this point in her career she has usually amassed the fair rewards of her talent in such measure as to enable her to invoke the assistance of a fashionable dressmaker in repressing the generosity or in concealing the parsimony of Nature. Whatever the outward shell may be, the inner woman falls into either one or other of these classes and acts accordingly. But between her origins and this goal of consecrated fame there lies a road along which the traffic is animated, gay flowers of romance nod invitingly in the adjacent meadows; there are thorny byways, but the stream of pilgrims in search of adventure flows on, to the delight of the disinterested spectator.

Her origins are as various as herself. Sometimes she springs into the literary arena like another Athena, fully armed, from the bosom of a family already famous in the academic groves and in the world of polite letters. More usually she begins in the traditional manner, befitting this great Republic, from the very bottom of the Jacob's ladder which leads right up to the heaven of Fame in New York. The romantic process of "making the grade" has an irresistible appeal for all citizens of these States, and so I prefer to dwell upon those careers which present analogies with the successes achieved in the stern world of commerce and industry by working from the bottom up. Let us contemplate once more the divine plan in Nature, whereby the grub evolves into a chrysalis and finally emerges as a butterfly of the Muses fanning her lovely wings in the warm breezes of admiration and flattery.

The literary lady comes, for preference, from the Middle West, where, as the experts tell us, the genius of American literature blossoms out of humble and often drab surroundings. Her family, certainly, had no pretensions of an æsthetic kind and was merely mildly amused by her girlish affection for the books obtainable at the Free Library and her vague ambition to be a poet. When she published some verses anonymously in the local newspaper they were not averse to confessing with some pride, at the Church socials and similar entertainments, that their little girl was the author. Against mothers who shared their daughters' conviction that the movies opened up a career for their looks, if not their talents, her mother urged the higher claims of literature for her own child. She, honest woman, had never trifled with the arts and knew no intellectual dalliance other than that which she occasionally enjoyed in "The Ladies' Home Journal," where she restricted her attention to its hints as to practical matters of the household, with a glance, now and then, at some of the magazine's more spectacular moral campaigns. By the time she could subside into a rocker on the front porch in the late afternoon the daily round and the trivial task had incapacitated her for active citizenship in the republic of letters. However, with a literary daughter on her hands she found herself inevitably assuming the responsibilities which the American man traditionally leaves to his women folk. Father, at all events, was entirely uninterested in the girl's career.

He could not afford to send her to a university, and so, to this day, she gazes a little enviously at the Phi Beta Kappa keys that adorn some of her contemporaries on state occasions, when such insignia are perhaps even more effective than good looks. She wasted a couple of years at an inferior college for women, a period of gloom lightened only by a growing consciousness of her own inspiration. She had left behind her the anonymity of the local press, and her signature was becoming familiar to the editors of magazines in the East. One genial member of that honorable profession, in particular, who viewed with a friendly sympathy all signs of intellectual activity west of Pittsburgh, returned her manuscripts but accompanied them with letters so friendly and stimulating that she found herself telling him all that troubled her ingenuous mind. Whereat he, scenting the possibilities of a story or two exposing the seamier side of American civilization, renewed his exhortations to her to write. She sent him several epigrams on love and marriage so excruciating in their cynicism that he could not but

acquiesce when she asked him to autograph her
copy of his early opus on Nietzsche. Meanwhile,
"The Bell Man," "Reedy's Mirror," "The Outlook"
and "The Midland" were printing her verses. With
her autographed Nietzsche in her valise and the
light of determination shining in her eyes she set
out for Chicago, the first station on her road to
glory.

A veil of discretion has been drawn over her brief
sojourn in that windy oasis, indiscreet though she
has always been in matters of less interest to the
literary historian. It was there that love first entered her life, and she gave to Amor what she had
doubtless intended for the Muses, but Amor, it
must be added, has since returned the compliment
a thousandfold. Love, it is true, smiled but to deceive, but in that deception was involved an education which remains the only effort of that kind
which she has ever made. Of course the hero was
a literary editor and a radical, so that it was a
liberal education, ranging from economics, feminism
and birth control to nights with the British poets
and expert advice in the polishing of lines and the
preparation of manuscript for the press. "Poetry"
had just begun to appear, and it was to the stern
scrutiny of its editors that the first offerings of her
now experienced Muse were submitted. I think the
note of exultant passion somewhat alarmed the cen-
sors, but finally she did appear in that "Magazine
of Verse."

At this stage the literary lady was a chrysalis
on the verge of self-realization. She could hear the
East a-calling, and she longed to be where the best
is like the worst. The gay romance of song had

waned, and literary Chicago itself seemed to have its eyes turned towards the East. Like another Pucelle, she hearkened to her Voices—editorial, chiefly—urging her to linger no longer but to pursue her quest to the very shores of the Atlantic. Her good mother, innocent of the craft and guile of the Evil One, rejoiced that her daughter had chosen literature rather than Hollywood, and the printed evidence of her success dried the tears which she might have shed over the loss of her child. The announcement of the latter's departure for New York, reënforced by quotations from the more laudatory and optimistic passages in the letters of the editorial sirens, was received with resignation slightly tinged with pride. And on the impulse of this latter emotion, a small contribution towards the pilgrim's progress was dispatched from the family purse.

Her first weeks in New York still seem like chapters from some fairy tale, so mysteriously did Fate move, its wonders to perform. Her Chicago letters of introduction at once admitted her into circles where high thinking and—when possible—not too plain living were the rule. She discovered on the part of sympathetic males an even greater disposition to be helpful than in Chicago, where her opportunities had been rather restricted by the exclusive insistence of passion. Now she was captain of her own soul, and her head was unbowed unless when she gracefully and deliberately inclined it to meet eyes that willingly lost themselves in hers. At studio parties she at once assumed a place of her own, and her victims, if insignificant, were numerous. She found that her work aroused an immediate response in those who had but recently emerged from the shelter of the universities. But she realized that ambition must be made of sterner stuff, so she made a judicious choice from her published and unpublished poems and set out to find a publisher.

It was then that she first used her knowledge of this man-made world to achieve a purpose other than the realization of her own tremulous soul. As she sat in the publisher's office, her eyelids drooping demurely, she became aware of a vast and powerful sympathy on his part with one so young, so inexperienced and so fair. She read to him one or two of those never-to-be-forgotten verses, in which she has recorded her ceaseless pursuit of Love that is forgotten almost as soon as it is born. She looked so frail, so simple, and that voice was an enchantment to an ear accustomed to a cynicism more carefully concealed because induced by a more authentic sophistication. The eternal struggle was on. A publisher actually held in his hands "youth's sweet-scented manuscript." The result, as she soon saw, was a foregone conclusion—she came, she saw and was published.

Long before that first little volume of verse was on the editorial tables, she had extended her operations to the editors themselves. She had only to present herself to receive the nicest welcome, usually followed by an invitation to lunch. How these luncheon parties of two dragged on, amidst the glare of much gilt, and the tawdry softness of red plush, intended to convey hints of Paris and the *beaux arts*. A cocktail or two always helped in the consideration of plans and manuscripts, and the wines were so well selected that she had to rely less upon sheer technique and could let nature do the rest. They were delightful and fruitful conferences, out of which came friendships that have survived even the pitiless publicity of her poetic versions of them. Nor was the ostensible purpose of the meetings forgotten, for out of them came the stimulus which eventually produced her book of prose— needless to say, a disingenuous chronicle of Middle Western inhibitions.

Meanwhile her fame as a poetess had grown, her not too frequent volumes were sure of an enthusiastic press, and doors opened to her as easily as hearts —more easily, in fact, when the hearts were feminine, for, like most of her sex, she believed that men understood her so much better than women. But her colleagues amongst her own sex had become acutely conscious of her existence. Her prowesses —in literature, needless to say—were duly listed in the Bulletin of the League of American Pen Women, and she recited her poems to the New York Poetry Society. It is at such functions that the peculiar exercise of all her talents can be most effectively studied. If a rival is actively present she can be relied upon to do whatever is necessary to create a diversion in her own favor, even to the extent of walking in late while another is reading. If called upon for a critical opinion of a rival's work she casts criticism to the winds and relies upon feminine intuition. Thus, she is never afraid to state in print that no authentic experience lies back of love poems other than her own. Her longer book-reviews are a serious matter, remaining long in the process of elucubration and becoming on publication subjects of respectful comment amongst her admiring friends. She is inclined to the opinion that once she has reviewed an author the last word has been said and further discussion is useless.

Although she writes but little now in the coterie magazines, she retains her girlish predilection for the young men who edit them and is guided by them in her appreciation of European literature. In Paris she is a familiar figure in those circles where expatriate genius takes advantage of the linguistic innocence of French printers to issue books containing obscenities unprintable in England or America. When she contributes a letter from abroad to an American periodical she displays the requisite recklessness in the misuse of French idiom, and her enthusiasms are strictly those of the little group with which she is in personal contact. A subtle problem is presented by her versions of foreign poetry, since it is not always possible to demonstrate that what passes for poetic license is really ignorance of the original. She relies, in such cases, upon her charm and upon the affecting habit which so many reviewers adopt of declaring the excellence of a translation, although unacquainted with the language from which it is made.

When measured in those years which, it seems, like great black oxen, tread the world where men of letters labor, her career has been as vertiginously rapid as the beat of passion in her poetry. But they have been years of plenty, of experiences so plentiful that she constantly vows her incapacity to remember them. Perhaps the skeptic might suggest that quality rather than quantity would have been the best mnemonics, but the insinuation is comparable only to the brushing of a clumsy thumb across the wings of a butterfly. She herself realizes that her life has been too crowded for measurement by ordinary standards. And so she has learnt to become gradually a little more aloof, less of a private delight and more of a public personage, already almost legendary. Even the professors now mention her quite casually as the greatest figure of her generation, and broadcasting stations transmit her poems, as naturally as if they were the words of a politician or the report of a boxing-match. Men, now older than when they first bade her to discourse for their enchantment, persuade themselves that they were not glamored by youth but by genius. Her marriage is spoken of with a mingling of relief and admiration at so bold a stroke.

The literary lady is nothing if she is not a woman. She has abandoned the chilling tradition of late Victorian feminism and is rapidly cured of her early affectation of clothing more masculine than feminine in its outline and texture. Naturally, the permanent acquisition of the male is by no means absent from her designs, although postponed until the move is the inevitable and only thing to do. If she has left anywhere on the road behind her some mute and inglorious first husband, he is properly pilloried in a ruthless novel of degraded domesticity. The man of destiny is more fortunate in being a later and more premeditated choice. She selects him usually from some walk in life as remote as possible from the hectic world of the arts. He has the solid virtues, the traditions broadening down from bank account to bank account, which are a guarantee of such security as is compatible with the artistic temperament. That is to say, his wife must be secure, not he. His fate is to be a member of that inverted Lucy Stone League of whose members it is said: "Oh, that is the husband of Miss So-and-So." When the worst comes to the worst, as it sometimes does, for change is the essence of her existence, then he has, at least, the satisfaction of obtaining a form of publicity undreamt of in the philosophy of his business friends. He gets on the front page of the newspapers, without an oil stain on his character.

3. A MID-WESTERN PORTRAIT

EVER since Chicago was declared the literary capital of America he has been coming East. The Middle Western intellectual, if ingratiating, is certainly not a modest fellow, and no sooner did he learn how important he was than he drew his own pragmatic conclusions. He decided that it would be wrong—nay, unpatriotic and un-American—to give to his own people what was obviously intended for mankind. There was a danger lest America should become hampered by a problem hitherto observed only in the West of Ireland, where the benevolent British government discovered what was termed Congested Districts, and proceeded to establish a Congested Districts Board to deal with the conditions resulting from a soil too poor to support the number of persons settled upon it. The Middle West threatened to become an intellectually Congested District with more literati to the acre than could live there in adequate comfort. And so the great hegira began, but for which, literature and journalism in New York could never have been what they are to-day.

They were a hardy and hard-headed breed who retraced the steps of their grandparents in their march towards the conquest of the East. On the long dark nights of Samhain, as Synge might have put it, when the wind does be whistling up Randolph Street and down Randolph Street, these sturdy men and women were grappling earnestly with the fruits of culture as dispensed by the University of Chicago, as sung by the percussionist music of Huneker's criticism, as garnered from the full-blooded admonitory encyclicals of H. L. Mencken. Under the benign tutelage of professors who reversed the natural laws of their species elsewhere by being less sinned against than sinning, a pagan generation uttered its barbaric yawps of joy, as it tumbled pell-mell into the delights of wine, woman and ideas—the three essentials of any genuine civilization. Oh, those great open spaces of the mind, where men are men like Stendhal and Stirner, Remy de Gourmont and Flaubert, Petronius and Artzibashef and women have an unending appetite for life and letters, in the cocktail combination of two parts life to one part letters, with a dash of absinthe—a heady but inspiring beverage.

"Laughing the stormy, husky, brawling laughter of Youth" the playboy of the Mid-Western World has tamed the seven-headed dragon of the Arts. He will invite the Muses to his studio parties and soon has his arm around their waists. His irreverence and self-confidence are irresistible, and he will as soon elucidate an obscure line in Pindar as transliterate the strange hieroglyphics of Thorstein Veblen; Beethoven and Stravinsky fill him with the same delight as Irving Berlin and George Gershwin. He is no respecter of persons and will discourse upon equal terms with Anatole France and Fanny Brice; Lord Dunsany's aristocratic rudeness has no terrors for him; he takes a brotherly interest in the sex-life of Dr. Sigmund Freud. His all-embracing humanity is his dominant characteristic. No man is a hero to the Middle West unless he is willing to submit to the familiarity which breeds respect, for beneath this surface roughness there is a profound belief in the artist, an endless curiosity and demand for creative ideas. But here is a short-sleeved æsthetic, impatient of pomp and circumstance, that cries Camerado with Whitmanesque good-fellowship, and utters the warning: abandon all dignity, ye who enter here.

Chicago being the nursery of this lusty breed, the Mid-Westerner naturally acquires something of its clangorous spaciousness, its wide horizon of the prairies. He looks tenderly upon a university against which even Upton Sinclair finds it difficult to maintain his goose-step thesis. If he begins by discovering American professors who are actually human beings, it is little wonder that he carries with him through all his later life that democratic conviction of his, that we are all just men and women under our skins, and does not exclude from this charitable assumption even the visiting English literary gent—much to the latter's discomfiture on certain historic occasions now inscribed in the city's literary annals. "The Hog Butcher for the World" and "The Nation's Freight Handler," he does not hesitate to slaughter dull decorum, and he receives the passing flow of celebrities, of seasonal crazes, of serious artists and astute charlatans, with a little of the baggage smasher's casual and sometimes destructive efficiency.

With Robert Herrick and Robert Morss Lovett as pillars of academic fire by day and Joe Roussel's table d'hôte a cloud of smoke by night, he made his pilgrimage into the Promised Land of art and of letters. Around the Frenchman's family board he sat for forty cents, absorbing food and wine and a vague atmosphere of that distant France whose prophets he had learned to read in dog-eared volumes of the *Mercure de France*. Remy de Gourmont was his greatest discovery since Nietzsche was revealed to him in the pioneering scripture of H. L. Mencken. From the *Livre des Masques* and Léautaud and Van Bever's anthology he extracted those names, Laforgue, Lautréamont and so forth, with which he still conjures up visions that have been transmitted to the younger New York æsthetes. His enthusiasms at this time were generous. He had seen "Poetry" and "'The Little Review" launched; in the Little Theatre Movement he had been spurred to action while the East was still awaiting the advent of the Washington Square Players. At Schlogl's foaming seidels of beer engendered the mood in which great thoughts are freely bandied; Mrs. Havelock Ellis came and comforted groups of radical thinkers whose advocacy of birth control was merely part of a general disposition to disrupt the home and make family life as diversified as it now appears in the transcripts of "Moon Calf" and "Many Marriages."

Schlogl's restaurant, now elevated to the dignity of a Middle Western Algonquin with round table and celebrities all complete, was then an eating place for impetuous and inspired youth. The tide of culture was flowing high and broke in frothy waves against the staunch slabs of the sunburnt West. Brieux and Tagore and Montessori glamored minds still innocent of the devilries of Jung and Freud, Guillaume Apollinaire had not yet displaced the old gods for whom James Huneker had prepared the

way in his "Iconoclasts" and "Egoists," and Theodore Dreiser, *in partibus infidelium*, had begun to
come into his own, and to stand forth to the world
as a sign and a portent of the great Middle Western
Renaissance. The book pages of the Chicago "Daily
News" and "Tribune" came into the hands of the
new generation and dimmed whatever remnants of
glory still clung to their New York rivals. At the
Dill Pickle, debates and lectures engaged the nights
of wondering rustics, cosmic mysteries, from free
verse to free love, were unfolded, and the Seven
Arts were jazzed up with saxophonic ecstasy. The
syncopated rhythm of Chicago's literary life dominated the gentler music of the older spheres, and
men raised their eyes to the heavens and beheld new
stars in the West. H. L. Mencken, chief of the
Wise Men of the East, greeted the birth of this other
babe, humbly born in that barn known, with characteristic irreverence for sacred things, as the Dill
Pickle, with tribute of frank incense and the myrrh
of his pungent prose.

Let us gaze for a last moment upon the Mid-
Western intellectual at this stage of his evolution,
for we shall not look upon his like again. He has
now reached his majority and has intimations of
immortality, as the roaring loom of time weaves for
him the vesture of metropolitan fame. He is the
self-made man of letters who awakes to find himself famous. His achievements have now reached
that point of obvious renown when even New York
editors are dimly aware of his existence and are
gradually arriving at the conclusion that he is just
the man they want. But those whom the gods wish
to destroy are first psycho-analyzed, so our stacker

of intellectual wheat must prepare himself for the sweets and usufructs of editorial life in New York, where every Chicagoan pleases and only the Easterner is vile, in the estimation of the publishers and newspaper owners. With the increase of his familiarity with the Tree of Knowledge and the fruits of Good and Evil, he had discerned in himself a curious unrest. Now that he had a secretary of his own he perhaps looked at her, and, behold, she was very good. Be that as it may, it was evident that his personality was becoming submerged in the humdrum depths of dreary domesticity, and, with the pioneering resolution of his people, he decided that the probe of psycho-analysis must enter his subconscious. The result more than justified the hopes he had conceived of this remarkable and accommodating science. As has so often happened since, after like inquiry, he got rid of his wife, and from that day he was inhibited no more.

The slogan of New York newspaperdom had now become, "Have you a little Mid-Westerner in your home?" The great migration had begun. Not all whose upturned glance beheld with awe the starry vault of Grand Central Station arrived trailing contracts of editorial glory. The vanguard of the invaders, equipped by their studies of the Latin and French poets, naturally gravitated to lucrative posts on magazines devoted to women's underwear or the publication of red-blooded fiction. But there straggled in the rear a strange band of roving adventurers and camp followers, unkempt and aggressive, who lived obscurely on the bounty of their more fortunate compatriots, despising them for the money which was plentiful enough to help them, and publishing devastating novels and sardonic and eccentric verse. Misunderstood geniuses, these, naturally convinced that criticism in America has reached the lowest depths of insensitiveness to the peculiar beauties of the art of which they alone are the true craftsmen. This art is compounded of the worst faults of the Parisian eccentrics of thirty years ago and a native Middle Western naïveté which delights in its own dismayed but fascinated astonishment at the perverse ironies of callous Nature. The inescapable fate of such as these is to lose themselves in the crowd of provincial cosmopolitans who get their typography from Paris and their ideas from Pittsburgh.

The fine flower of the Middle West makes no such retreat from the metaphorical Moscow of its ambition. If he has exchanged the more or less placid waters of Lake Michigan for the salt breezes blowing in from the dolorous sea, it is because he has come East with the same determination as his grandfather went West. His rugged soul is not saddened nor his indomitable spirit broken by the five-inch thick carpet, the mahogany, glass-covered and immaculate desk, the dazzling array of bell-buttons and ever-sharpened pencils within easy reach of his manicured hand, as he carefully selects the coming patterns for modish tailor-mades. There is the glint of vigorous youth in his eye as he approves the captions written for the photographs of celebrities by some charming young thing arrayed in such glory as to suggest the gravest doubts, until one discovers that she is the daughter of God-fearing parents, who simply cannot understand why she prefers the ardors and endurances of the magazine world to the shelter of a millionaire's home. His easy familiarity with the great world of letters, originally responsible for his being selected so aptly to fill his present post, is not by any means a memoir of his dead life. It enables him to justify his existence by making suggestions for the purchase of great fiction by hands no less eminent than those of Arnold Bennett, Ethel M. Dell and H. G. Wells or, in his more intellectual flights, even an article on the marriage problem by George Bernard Shaw.

Not only does his background of intensive culture assist him in the discharge of his editorial duties by providing him with the knowledge out of which such great enterprise alone can spring, it also stands him socially in good stead. In his apotheosis as the arbiter of all elegancies the Mid-Westerner is called upon for social functions undreamed of in the philosophy of his rude forefathers. As the chairman at a Colony Club literary afternoon he finds that he can draw upon the accumulated wisdom of the days when he wrote for "The Little Review," or the less remote era when his book page supplied the New York publishers with the maximum of quotable material. On more festive occasions, when a dinner party sees him in faultless linen and the most ravishing of dress clothes, achieving the almost poetic dreams of Beau Nash himself, his conversation is amply nourished on the merest crumbs from the old feasts of reason at Joe Roussel's and Schlogl's. When he sits with appropriate seriousness at important first nights, his boredom is tempered by fond memories of the heroic days when he took the drama seriously and was an active worker in the little theater group back home. In brief, he reaps the rewards of a well-spent youth.

The divine fire, moreover, still burns in his veins, and at times he succumbs to the old lure, renouncing the treasures at which moth and rust can get for the more insubstantial but purer joys of a literary editorship. Away from the gaudy decorations and seductive softness of the fashionable magazine editor's sanctum, he breathes the old smell of printer's ink, his nostrils quiver sensitively, mayhap a tear dims his eye as he sees the huge bales of paper being unloaded in the street below his window. The rattle of typewriters is around him, the strident shouts of an amplifier in the radio department stir up some atavistic response in the newspaperman that lives on in him. He rolls up his shirt sleeves, assures himself that the cuspidor is within convenient range, and sets out to conquer new fields. The newspaper is his spiritual home; here he can be truly himself, and New York in due course discovers that a new comet has swum into its ken. This intensely personal note, this ravenous appetite for all the arts, this style that launched a thousand tiffs, this prodigious energy, announce a literary editor who is like a theme for Carl Sandburg's poetry: "Half-naked, sweating, proud to be Hog Butcher, Tool Maker, Stacker of Wheat, Player with Railroads, and Freight Handler." So he seems, by analogy, when compared with his effete colleagues. His daily life is an open book for all to read, and likewise that of his friends, who live in a state of delighted terror, as the record of their intellectual, amorous and alcoholic indiscretions is spread out for the bewilderment of the multitude. He gives cocktail parties to the Muses, has them swaying to the ululations of his literary saxophone, and puts pep and punch into the adventures of his mind amongst masterpieces. His week is one of Bach and Bacardi, Martinis and D'Annunzio, Old Testament exegesis and jazz, Marcel Proust and Paul Elmer More. He is the Blind Bow-boy of literature; his shafts fall upon the just and unjust alike.

These crowded hours of obviously glorious life might mean the whole sum of existence to the ordinary man of letters. The Mid-Westerner is made of sterner stuff; his final consummation is not yet, the supreme incarnation of the spirit that broods over the lonely prairie. That moment comes when he confronts us as a novelist, a successful novelist, of course, for his preliminary skirmishes need not detain us. They are usually the painful record of belated adolescence groping and clambering out of the sex morass, sinister pictures of deflected desires and thwarted passions, expressed in a prose that is as muddled and inarticulate as the author's characters themselves. When he finally achieves world fame, it is with a masterpiece peculiarly his own. It is written with all the snap of high-grade advertising, but it satirizes the advertiser and his customers; it is an indictment of the American bourgeoisie drawn up in terms of perfect Philistinism; it is the most ingenious of all devices for tickling the palate of the mob, a lampoon upon themselves by one of themselves; the distorting mirror is held up to Nature by a prestidigitator who cunningly contrives his trick so that the reflection is never that of the beholder. To the sale of this work the transcendent child of the golden Middle West

brings all the technique of expert salesmanship. He
organizes his own advertising campaign and boosts
literature much as the realtors of his native burgh
put over their campaigns for choice lots and desirable homes.

To this end the inscrutable laws of the Universe
have been at work, slowly and deviously evolving
a precious type to set in the diadem of our glorious
civilization. Nature with her customary prodigality seems to scatter and waste the material, the energies which have gone into this creative process.
Finite man may turn over with a melancholy sigh
a file of "The Little Review" and draw disconsolate
conclusions from the contrast between the present
position and the early promise of many whose names
adorn that Middle Western roll of honor. He who
wrote, with all the rapture of youthful genius, poems
and prose that stirred the imagination now edits
in luxury photographs of mannequins; she whose
witty and irreverent fantasies were the herald of
an alert and civilized sense of humor is now the
disgruntled author of unread and unreadable novels
of unwashed sinks and domestic strife. But there
is a divine purpose in Nature, we are reminded,
when the resplendent and vociferous Mid-Western
novelist challenges us with his success on both sides
of the Atlantic at the hands of all classes of readers.
The rough-hewn ends of the movement have been
shaped by the divinity concerned. The result is
Brighter and Better Babbitts.

4. A LITERARY ENTHUSIAST

SHE is the mainstay of the republic of letters, the hand that rocks the literary cradle and rules the world. Hers is a career open to the talents of Everywoman; no feminist propaganda has been necessary to prepare the way for her, she dates her ancestry back to the night beneath the stars in Eden, when Eve's bright eyes pleaded with Adam to show her what he had written, to recite his verses to her. Down through the ages she has existed. She was Egeria in ancient Rome and the Marquise de Rambouillet in the days of the Précieuses; the autographs which she wrested from coy Egyptian poetasters doubtless slumber mongst the papyri of Tut-Ankh-Amen, and, I suspect that Moses presented her with an original signed tablet on which he had engraved the ten commandments. She is outside of time and space, as it were, for she can be herself in the obese years of maturity and in the querulous last days of old age, no less effectively—sometimes even more so—than in the springtime of youth. The literary enthusiast's is not a seasonal occupation. It is the work of a lifetime.

In this Land of Opportunity, needless to say, her opportunities are infinite, and as infinite is the variety of her incarnations. Her first intimations of this particular form of immortality came to her in college, when what seemed to her a comparatively human professor of English literature suddenly lighted up the dreary class-room hours devoted to the art of beautiful letters.   The gentleman presented no characteristics unusual to his species, when examined in the harsh light of experience and with scientific detachment.   He had written the usual thesis on the use of the semicolon in English prior to Beowulf, or some similar topic, and, when subjected to the soothing effects of malt liquor, he would confess that he had always believed there must be something in Whitman to justify the enthusiasm of Europeans, but he considered it safer to reserve that opinion for private consumption amongst friends.   In the eyes of our embryonic literary enthusiast he had, however, the glamor of authorship.   While at Oxford, as a Rhodes scholar, he had perpetrated, with the connivance of the obliging B. H. Blackwell, a little book of verse, which was listed after his name in "Who's Who," sharing all the honors with the learned thesis already mentioned.   The book was long since out of print, so that it enjoyed in a special degree the enchantment of distance.

Distant, but without any enchantment, was the attitude of the eminent pedagogue's wife, who viewed with a suspicious eye the flutterings of the young ladies about their first intellectual hero. This stimulus was sufficient to spur the ambitions of the enthusiast, who there and then acquired that manner with the wives of her idols which she has carried with her all through life.   Her refusal to be deterred, nay, the very impetus given to her hovering illusions, were the authentic marks of her fitness for the career in which she was to become famous, after a fashion.   This was the ordeal by fire through which she passed, while others failed to stand the supreme test, and, thus tempered, she accepted her destiny. Her religion is essentially anthropomorphous, a biological necessity, so to speak, as she realized when Nature cunningly provided the protective coloring and demonstrated the glorious process whereby the organism adapts itself to its environment. The literary enthusiast is an excellent example of the survival of the fittest.

With such a mentor she very naturally developed that rudimentary knowledge of literature which is her one intellectual asset in the struggle for social life. None was so industrious as she in obeying the directions of her master's voice; her rapt gaze encountered his as he surveyed his class, and she was always the first to ask a question and to receive with appropriate eagerness the words of æsthetic wisdom which followed. When writing her compositions she would see his face before her, and it was for his sake that she achieved an almost convincing interest in the more intellectual poems of Tennyson, and professed herself deeply moved by the platitudes of Santayana which, she gathered, were real literature. Her craving for books other than those in her prescribed courses supplied many opportunities for talks which could not but bring closer together the minds of master and disciple. He, beholding an attractive young woman who obviously adored him respectfully, could not but feel that he would be failing in his duty to himself and to the cause of higher education were he to neglect any opportunity of giving her his counsel and the benefit of his learning.

He had got to the point of showing her his early

poems, and had actually noted within his bosom the stirrings of a Muse whom he had buried long ago beneath the dust of useless erudition.   One day— it must have been in spring—when they were alone in the deserted class-room, he produced some lines between which she read what his lips had refused to speak.   He confessed that she had inspired him, and that she was one of those women who are destined to call forth the best that is in a man, to foster the arts and to be an Influence.   He did not become as specific as she hoped, for which his wife was blamed.   But the truth is, he became suddenly conscious of the enormous complications yawning like an abyss in front of him.   He saw himself in flight from a board of God-fearing trustees, he had visions of front page newspaper stories, the inevitable arrival in New York, the unsubstantial aid of radical editors, his inability to shine in contrast with gaudier rivals in Greenwich Village.   He made the great refusal, like Dante's Pope, and, like Paolo and Francesca, but for exactly the opposite reasons, that day they read no more.

Thus, by an apparently cruel but actually benign dispensation of inscrutable Fate the literary enthusiast came to New York, not in the wake of a scandal-bedraggled professor, but as the wife of a rising young lawyer, as untroubled by artistic preoccupations as by the impecuniosity which is the lot of those who think the world well lost for Art.   She recovered from the girlish illusion of her college days, having seen other men and other manners in the meantime.   But the divine fire kindled by that humble Academic flint burned with what she might have termed a clear, steady flame.   She was pos-

sessed by an endless capacity for the ecstasies of
culture, and once her own life was fixed upon a
stable basis, she began to fulfill her mission. Her
ideal husband was considerably flattered by his
wife's familiarity with refined literature and ef-
faced himself from that part of her existence devoted to the arts and their practitioners. She was
the honorary secretary of several clubs for the cultivation of literature, and could be counted upon
to act as a committee member or patroness, whenever any foreign genius felt drawn to deliver his
message on these shores.

In fashionable circles, on the fringe of literary
life, she passed as an authority upon all modern
movements, and her allusions to the topical interests of the moment were always effective. The
scope of her patter ran from Brieux to Marcel
Proust, and in season her talk was of Montessori
and Barbusse, of Sinclair Lewis and Sherwood Anderson, of Ouspensky and Ronald Firbank. She
would have liked to acquire a copy of "Ulysses,"
but the cost seemed excessive for a mere book.
Moreover, she had read the last chapter and feared
its effect upon the untutored mind of her red-
blooded spouse, unaccustomed as he was to public
peeping at the secrets of the alcove, rendered possible by the beneficent influence of psycho-analysis,
which had supplied the English-speaking world
with a scientific jargon to cover certain lacunæ in
its vocabulary, thereby making sex discussion a polite accomplishment. She had a charge account at
several of the little bookshops which specialized in
the importation of English books, for she knew it
was the right thing to be seen with the London

editions of Katherine Mansfield and Virginia
Woolff under her arm. On her table one always
found "The Dial," the more freakish numbers of
"The Little Review," and "The London Mercury."
She had met the sterner intellectuals who guided the
destinies of the first of these magazines, when on an
intellectual slumming party in Greenwich Village.
Her introduction of Mr. J. C. Squire at the Colony
Club remains one of her proudest memories.

The literary enthusiast shows her real caliber
where lectures are concerned. She is usually the
person delegated to approach the lion who is to
perform, and who has not succumbed to her blan-
dishments? Her voice comes over the telephone
announcing, "You don't know me, Mr. So-and-So,
but I have followed your work with great interest.
Our Club is most anxious to have you give us a
little talk on any subject you care to choose. I am
sorry we have no funds on which to draw in such
cases, but we will have cards printed with your
name and give you a lot of publicity." It is she
who warmly grasps the lecturer's hand, and, if he
is a novelist, assures him that she greatly enjoyed
his series of articles on Einstein in "Good House-
keeping." To the critic whose literary articles are
the cherished feature of one of the austere monthlies
she will express her intense pleasure in his wonderful novel about a man and a woman who for-
sook the world and in the great open spaces found
themselves. If the meeting takes place in one of
the obscurer literary slums, she reminds the speaker
of her intimacy with the great by casual references
to what Mr. Hugh Walpole told her, and a friendly

allusion to the personal charm of Miss Rebecca West.

When she is a spectator, her passive rôle is converted into an active one the moment an opportunity occurs. When the subject is opened for general discussion, it is she who first catches the chairman's eye and holds the floor in irrelevant discourse. She likes to ask Signor Pirandello what he thinks of sex in American literature and whether he has read Waldo Frank. From John Drinkwater or Alfred Noyes she is consumed with a desire to learn the true significance of James Joyce and Marcel Proust. No visiting Englishman can ever sufficiently satisfy her curiosity concerning the private life and mythical amours of Mr. George Moore. No sooner have the proceedings terminated than she has rushed up to the platform to thank the lecturer personally and to thrust a book into his hands for his autograph. This is a more certain and economical method than sending books by mail with a request for an inscription—so many authors are now reluctant to comply with such demands. If she has paid for a seat at a Book and Play lunch, the trophy of an autograph is, in some measure, a return on her investment. Not that she thinks of the matter in sordid terms. Her preoccupations are fundamentally æsthetic. Going down in the elevator after one of these functions, she declared that Mr. J. C. Squire did not look a bit like a poet. That is the only demonstration of dissatisfaction she has been known to make. The literary enthusiast is not by nature critical.

Her genius lies in her infinite capacity for taking

pains to keep in the swim. Her reading is conducted on the principle of a Barmecide feast. "What do you think of Sherwood Anderson's new book?" "Do you really believe that Rose Macaulay is a great writer?" "Isn't the translation of Paul Morand wonderful?" Such is her table-talk, and the unwary usually fall into the trap, explaining, perhaps, that "Many Marriages" is a dreadful anticlimax to "Winesburg, Ohio," that "What Not" and "Potterism" were much better than "Told by an Idiot," that "Open all Night" contains errors for which a schoolboy would be punished—only to discover that the questioner has read none of these authors and is simply an echo awaiting other echoes. Any innovation in the responses produces puzzled alarm. Her greatest guides are the columnists who are marked off from all other writers, so far as she is concerned, in the sense that they alone are actually read by her. She always knows just exactly what Heywood Broun and F. P. A. like, and such fragments of their domestic life as they care to confide to the public. Burton Rascoe's Day Book is this child's guide to knowledge of literary life in New York. From that ingenuous chronicle she has gleaned more facts than from "The Outline of History" and "The Story of Mankind" which repose on her book shelves, unread, but—in their day—passionately discussed. When she wishes to see her Shelleys plain, to witness in the flesh what has diverted her morning meditations for many a day, she lunches at the Algonquin. In the lobby as she hovers near the barrier of red plush with which the Hellenic George, appropriately born in sight of Parnassus, bars access to the inner temple, she is already visibly impressed by her surroundings. She wonders what is the precise place in the literary hierarchy of all these feminine legs flaunting generously their silken contours, as their owners loll voluptuously or provocatively upon couches and in armchairs. Are they the Muses of the literati whose gastronomical activities she has come to contemplate? The horizon seems filled with flamboyant stockings. Is this a literary leg-show?

But soon she is negotiated past the thin red line of plush and is seated within the very shrine itself where, under the guidance of one of the initiated, she drinks in the glory of the scene. The Round Table is naturally the axis of her world, and she gazes a little enviously at those members of her sex who sit familiarly with the Olympians. The men, she confides, are not so handsome as Rudolph Valentino or Richard Barthelmess, who have been pointed out to her at a neighboring table, but they look "so interesting." F. P. A., like some exotic bird from Galápagos, with an enormous cigar in the corner of his mouth; Heywood Broun, with the lumbering roll of some pachydermatous animal; Alexander Woollcott, conveying somehow the impression of an irrepressible hoyden; the gargoyle figure of an impresario who knows what the public does not want and cannot understand and makes a fortune by providing it; the collegiate countenance of the youthful sage of Brooklyn, as he toys with a glass of milk, the unheavenly twins of comedy, musical and otherwise, in whose satire a mirror has been held up to the literary enthusiast in vain. Her senses swoon in the presence of these incarnations of her idols. For a moment or two her fascinated gaze wanders around the mirrors of the Algonquin, reflecting a scene unparalleled in the simple annals of this rude Republic.

Here is the ante-room of the hall of fame, where wit and intellect and beauty congregate, with nothing to screen them from the vulgar world but that symbolic rope of plush, which lifts ever and anon to admit some other member of the Times Square Country Club: Carl van Vechten, as feline as the tiger in the house. "That's the author of 'The Blind Bow-boy,'" the visitor learns with a little shock at the memory of such perversities; and there is Elinor Wylie, whose "Jennifer Lorn" is quite the thing to speak about; and the blindest bow-boy of them all, divine in his impartial indiscretion, Burton Rascoe, fortunately accompanied by the authentic Hazel of his Day Book; Gertrude Atherton, too,—even the literary enthusiast has read "Black Oxen," its interest transcends that of mere literature to Everywoman, and takes on an additional significance from the author's youthful presence; and Joseph Hergesheimer, beaming behind enormous spectacles, crowing like some huge baby who finds himself on the nursery floor of life surrounded by all the toys and sweets he craves; Scott Fitzgerald, and his radiant young wife, still this side of paradise, the flapper and the philosopher of the Jazz Age. Everywhere a celebrity, if only such as go unhonored and unsung outside the pages of "Broadway Brevities," where there are always some so poor to do them reverence. After such a glorious lunch hour of crowded life, the literary enthusiast passes, as one in a dream, out through that lobby where feminine legs have forgotten more than Herrick ever knew about the tempestuous petticoat.

Now the New York "World" can never be too much with her. The literary enthusiast speaks as one having the authority of personal revelation. For a while she may actually become a novice of the Algonquin Order, a humble neophyte at the altar of Fame. With the passage of time, these memories also join others of her dead life. God has been good, and her husband, now a balder and wiser man, has built the house with many mansions, worthy of a lady with salon propensities and a protective manner towards budding poets. The honorable poverty of the true artist never appeals in vain to this munificence, especially if it is young and prepossessing and helplessly masculine. Magazines devoted to the elusive art of the sonnet live upon her bounty, wild-eyed geniuses, with faded wives in Reno submitting to the inevitable, encamp upon her estate, and the bonds of holy matrimony, already frayed, snap dramatically during her parties. Her drawing-room has witnessed the reading of more bad verse than is dreamed of in the philosophy of the æsthetic reviews.

Obese and, oh, so kind, she ends her days as the Medici of the mediocre. Books bearing the imprint of unknown firms are dedicated to her, and ingenuous poetasters arise and call her blessed. Her success with women still bears the marks of her first challenge, and one notices the poetesses who adorn her recitals tend to a non-committal plainness, a depressing quality of spurious youth achieved by a combination of girlish draperies and arid spinster-

hood. The botched, the thwarted and the conscious
charlatans surround her, her husband's money com-
mands the respect which only these can give; except
by accident, no genuine artistic personality comes
within her purview. She sometimes captures, more
by luck than cunning, some tenth-rate foreigner,
who accepts her hospitality in good faith and is
measured by his subsequent behavior. The thoroughly parasitic arrange to live, like the native
larvæ, at her expense indefinitely. Such are the
last glories which her eyes behold, the phosphores-
cent gleams of decay are the simulacrum of the
haloes which once dazzled the literary enthusiast.

5. A MODERN MAECENAS

THE modern Maecenas is a two-headed monster or, in politer image, a Janus whose two faces represent the publisher and the bookseller, the twin patrons of literature in this era of democracy. The denizen of Grub Street to-day knows his patron as a dual personality, a Jekyll and Hyde, whose incarnations are revealed to him separately, although he suspects them of a closer identity than ostensibly appears. This composite being is not every publisher and bookseller, nor does it play Maecenas to every author. In order to study the phenomenon, it is essential that all irrelevant and distracting elements be eliminated. The writer whose works are shipped by the carload depends upon the pleasure and good will of none other than the great god Demos himself, and the functions of publisher and bookseller are essentially those of a servant both to the mob and its master. Maecenas becomes incarnate only to those who labor in the more modest fields of authentic literature and learning, and whose need places them in a position corresponding to that of author and patron in the old unregenerate days of unenlightenment. They have nothing to offer the wholesale fiction merchants, and their wares require more delicate handling than that vouchsafed by the bobbed-haired ruminants of the department stores.

For a new need benign Nature creates a new organ, and thus the hapless victims of the spread of education and knowledge are not left friendless

and unsuccored. Having striven for the best part
of a century to substitute illiterates who can read
and vote and make their mark upon history and
public taste for illiterates who could just make their
mark, and were rarely disturbed from their natural
avocations even to do that, having popularized the
goose that laid the once golden eggs of education,
we have now to protect the educators from the educated. In the eternal recurrence of things the
literati thus find themselves once more dependent
upon the bounty and benevolence of an individual
or group of persons endowed either with enough
money or enough taste to permit of their indulging
in pleasures undreamed of in the philosophy of the
herd. The modern Maecenas has come forward to
discharge the duties once undertaken by Lorenzo de
Medici and his like, and publishing and bookselling
have been adapted accordingly.

Naturally, one must not expect from the patron
of to-day anything of the magnificence and splendor
of a Renaissance lord, nor even the relative dis-
interestedness of a Lord Chesterfield lending his aid
to Samuel Johnson. The author nowadays who
seeks relief from the harsh laws of commercial
publishing turns away from those two conventional
institutions, the fiction factory where nothing less
than a sale of half a million copies entitles a book
to house room and those old and stately but formal
organizations where many generations of tradition
create an atmosphere of aloofness, something of the
coldness peculiar to the State, "that coldest of cold
monsters," as Nietzsche termed it. The one is too
crass and sordid, the other too institutional to play
the part assigned by an all-seeing providence to the

Medicis of our time. Human warmth, or at least the personal note, is the indication which is sought by those who hope to shelter beneath the favor of a patron.

It is at this point that the publishing face of Janus smiles upon the seekers after the immortality of letters. Instead of waiting in an unprepossessing but business-like ante-room, only to transact one's affairs with an impersonal assistant without plenary powers, one lingers, if at all, in some suave and seductive chamber where the passage of time is imperceptible. The literary Lotos-eater sits beguiled by softly shaded lamps, gaudy batiks, and a dazzling display of the most cultured and æsthetic publications. Instead of vulgar magazines in coarse leather covers, reminiscent of free libraries or English railway guides, one sees esoteric importations from every corner of Europe, and while one's heels sink into a carpet six inches thick, the eye beholds the wonders of Dadaist prose from Finland, or a complete file of the artiest and most unread American magazines published in Paris. The furnishings are a cross between a library and a boudoir in a really up-to-date movie. It becomes evident that the telephone girl is a graduate of Barnard, and the limousines of the staff, as they line up outside the office at half past five, suggest the curb in front of the New Amsterdam Theatre during a rehearsal of the Ziegfeld "Follies." The resplendent creatures who flit about have obviously given to literature what was intended for the glorification of the American girl:

> There is sweet music here that softer falls
> Than petals from blown roses on the grass.

Thus "propt on beds of amaranth and moly," the
innocent visitor is awakened from his reverie of
Lotos Land by a secretary arrayed in such glory as
no Solomon of literature could afford, breathing an
air of such friendliness and refinement, such odors
of Guerlain as make the senses swoon, that the
drawing-room effect is completed.   It is almost
without any emotion of surprise that the postulant
finds he is to be admitted into the presence of the
publisher himself, the host, rather, who is too well
bred to delegate the welcoming of his guests to a
subordinate.   The patron rises with the most pleasant smile, introduces the secretary as his assistant,
and soon all three are engaged in the happiest conversation.   The office is everything that a gentleman's library ought to be; the only implement be-
traying the dark shadow of business is one of those
mysterious, multicolored indexes in which little
pieces of gelatine are moved about from time to
time in obedience to the laws of some obscure
domino game.   A silver water bottle and two small
glasses of purest crystal repose on a tray.   Imported
cigarettes are produced, while the assistant from a
small gold case supplies herself with one whose
fantastic wrapping matches her costume, itself an
adorable creation from the Maison Simone, while
the silk tip cunningly matches the tender hue of
her silk stockings from Javotte's.   More discreetly
concealed than these, a cellar of carefully selected
ingredients provides, on occasion, unlawful refreshment for favored members of the publishing family.

Family, in effect, is the note of the new order.
The formal "Mr." or "Miss" is reserved for unpopular intruders, backsliders who have failed to

justify the confidence reposed in them, or the newest arrival who, hearing the constant allusions to authors by their Christian names, at once realizes that he has left behind him the cruel dispensation of commerce, and aspires to be affectionately addressed as one who is among friends. This interview, the first of many, prepares the way of initiation, the beginnings of a great friendship—on a royalty basis to be sure, but the transaction is enveloped in such attentions and pledges of good fellowship that the author is just vaguely reminded of his publisher, somewhat in the manner of a patient in the dentist's chair who has had a local anæsthetic and feels only a numb pain. The friends of the family are as charming as the host; if there are those jealousies which reveal themselves frankly in places where the nature of the literary gent is red in claw and fang, here that feminine affection which enables rival ladies to kiss on meeting is practiced by coaxing favorites. In this modern king's household there are many courtiers for the royal favor; court intrigues may lead to the destruction of rising reputations which cannot be injured by the old-fashioned method of wire-pulling in the press.

The poet in the palace, if he has the privileges of a status not obtainable elsewhere, incurs also dangers which do not threaten the writer who has a publisher only and not a patron. The enervating atmosphere of this court society is such that intrigue and rivalry are not confined to the sex traditionally credited with such weapons as are known in the vernacular as "cattishness." The women perhaps dismay the impartial observer by the ease with which their intuitions are mistaken for knowledge, in matters where expert opinion is required, but the patron is swayed more often by the more unexpected insinuations of the kind of man that men forget. The newly initiated, however, do not encounter this impalpable influence, if for no other reason, because no book has yet been published to dim the brightness of the scene. Long before the manuscript has been submitted to the butchery of the printers, the author has been fully received into the circle of the intimates; he is enjoying the delights of patronage, and the association of others like himself, who have emerged into the bright light of fame after secluded labors encouraged by the benevolence of Maecenas. As he sits in preliminary consultation with well-groomed publicity experts, furnishing such material as will create for him a personality which he may not have; as he smiles over his fourth cocktail at the now more seductive than ever secretary, as he participates in all that charming agitation preceding actual publication, when the combination of business and pleasure, of the shrewdest merchandising and the most disinterested geniality, reaches its apogee—then, indeed, memories of happy days at college crowd the excited brain, and the author murmurs, as he thinks of his transcendent publisher and friend, the immortal lines to the archetype of all patrons:

> quodsi me lyricis vatibus inseris,
> sublimi feriam sidera vertice.*

* For those whose Latin is as shaky as Shakespeare's, and who have no dictionary of quotations within reach, I translate:

> "But if you rank me among lyric bards
> With exalted head I shall touch the stars."

While his "exalted head" still touches the stars the author now becomes familiar with the other face of Janus, the bookseller. As every publisher is not Maecenas, neither is every vendor of books. The bookseller as patron must be as carefully distinguished from his conventional colleagues in the trade as was the publisher who transcends the mere wholesaling of raw material. By their books ye shall know them. The little book shops, the corner book shops, the neighborhood book shops, the shops that invoke the sign of fabulous birds and mythical animals, or somehow contrive to suggest an air of exoticism or esoteric fantasy—these do not compete with the common book stores of the plain people. Do not ask them for copies of "The Cross Word Puzzle Book" or the inspirational works of eminent popular philosophers; New Thought they do not trifle with, unless when it professes to elucidate the mysteries of sex. Best sellers are as unwelcome as those energetic gentlemen who call to offer an attractive line of stationery and fancy goods, and depart wondering what the book business is coming to, when sealing wax, calendars, birthday cards, and notepaper are not regarded as the backbone of an honorable commerce. It would be not only indiscreet but indecorous to enumerate the estimable authors who never rest upon the shelves of these establishments, and who, at best, pass through ignominiously as transients procured to the order of some customer as yet unacquainted with the delights of true culture.

In his book-selling capacity the modern Maecenas is as conscious of his duty to letters as he is in his capacity as publisher. He is in more direct contact with the reader and so his patronage extends not only to the author but to the public. Whether by a process of collusion or natural evolution, his shop, like the publisher's office, contrives to disguise its harsher commercial contours. The same shaded lamps are visible, the same imported magazines; and lounge chairs frequently invite that dalliance for which there is no place in the ordinary store. Usually, there are representatives of that resplendent sex whose presence dazzles the postulants who wait in the publisher's ante-chamber, perhaps not quite so modishly gowned but equipped, nevertheless, for the task of feminizing the humanities. Horn-rimmed glasses are worn with bewitching effect, and gazelle-like ankles flash, as fair handmaidens of learning trip to and fro from the shelves, proffering enthusiastic advice as to authors to be collected, and displaying a properly cultivated appreciation—with no trace of Puritan furtiveness—of the lewder passages in "Jurgen" and "Mademoiselle de Maupin." "Ulysses," of course, is discussed and recommended as part of the season's entertainment, lost in an enthusiasm which embraces "Antic Hay," "The Genius," and "Prancing Nigger." Those who were introduced to James Joyce while holidaying in Paris become serious acolytes. The others just rank him as one of the many who enable them to dabble conversationally upon the edge of topics previously obscured in the jargon of psycho-analysis.

The author who can enter the general book store and depart unrecognized and unsung finds in the little book shop that friendly recognition, that atmosphere of appreciation for which Maecenas has

prepared him. He finds that the two faces of Janus
are smiling, unless he be so unfortunate as to choose
a shop where his work has failed to come up to the
severe standard usually imposed. Then he has his
revenge, however, by alluding to a rival establishment and declaring in tones of condescending assurance: "My book is selling very well, *wherever it is
displayed.*" Whereupon the recalcitrant, but diplomatic, bookseller endeavors to convey the impression that all the others, having been piled up in a
prominent place, have been sold. Usually, however, these contretemps do not occur. The patron
bookseller has so well adjusted his authors, books,
and customers that they are all like one great happy
family. A translator may linger while a lady pur-
chaser descants upon the praiseworthy freedom with
which he has preserved in English those passages
whose Gallic salt had deterred all his predecessors.
Without knowing each other both writer and reader
leave the benevolent presence of the bookseller feeling that he is discharging a noble duty to the community. The learning of his customers is demon-
strably equal only to their discrimination.

If he is the author's friend, he is also the guide
and counselor of his clients. According to the sex
of the latter, the little book shop knows how to
wean them away from a too confiding faith in
the judgment of all-too-human columnists. Never
could the eternal lure of youth be more beautifully
sublimated than through the literary salesmanship
of a woman bent upon bringing to Lytton Strachey
and Michael Arlen a man who has heretofore bowed
down in his blindness to idols of wood and stone,
believing perhaps that in reading "Babbitt" he had

scaled the rarefied heights of sophisticated literature. What could be more admirable, more typical
of man's indomitable spirit, than the career of a
red-blooded American citizen who turns his back
on Wall Street in order to develop in cultivated
women a predilection for imported English first
editions, and an appreciation for the efforts of the
subtler and more perverse geniuses native to this
Republic? Women whose charge accounts at one
time were confined to household expenses and personal adornment, with perhaps a restaurant or two,
now acquire culture on a credit generously extended
by the new patron of hard-working authors.

The little book shop inevitably becomes a center
for the advancement of learning and the development of those higher faculties in mankind which,
it is said, distinguish us from the anterior members
of the animal kingdom. The walls are adorned
with playbills of subterranean theaters, circulars so-
liciting subscriptions for the magazines of all the
cliques, and even advertisements of studios to shelter the brainworker. The hovering authors move
about in sight of the traps set for them with the
innocence of domestic fowl. They are like those
tame pheasants which are shot by royalty when
beaters drive the unwitting birds into the air within
easy reach of the exalted sportsmen. Sooner or
later they agree to give a little talk to a select few,
chosen from the more influential supporters of the
establishment. When the patroness has reached
years of such discretion as enforces the wisdom of
literary monogamy, she leaves to more slender and
superficially enthusiastic assistants the daily round
of sublimation by way of first editions and cognate

topics. Within her breast burn deeper fires which flare up periodically in an all-excluding and all-consuming devotion to one author. His writings become the gospel, and he is not infrequently the willing victim of the lecture passion.

The intimate note of the shop is accentuated for the occasion, the comfortable wicker chairs are reserved for the great man and the privileged initiates, and upon uncomfortable hired chairs an adoring herd is huddled, as though cowering before the storm of eloquence which is imminent. Generally a poet who will read his verses is the attraction, but they, as a rule, are the helpless and defenseless victims of their divine calling. They might just as well be imposed upon here as elsewhere; it is their fate, since literature has been thrown to the people by the Cæsars of popular education. More peculiarly the product of this special environment is the prose writer who takes a special pleasure in this opportunity of airing his hollow ideas, which are indistinguishable from the platitudes of the syndicated philosophers scorned by this critical audience, save in so far as they are incomprehensible. A pleasant career is thus opened to those male charmers who make up for the paucity of their intelligence by the wealth of their admiration for the admiration of women. When one of the least of these can be persuaded to discourse upon some such topic as "Fourth Dimensional Love," refined women are rewarded for their abdication before the wantonly successful provocation of a younger generation also engaged in the cultivation of literature and its makers.

These relaxations of the patrons, with the intoxi-

cation corresponding to the more material inebria-
tion already referred to, must not deceive us as to
the importance of the dual rôle which is played by
the twin Maecenas of democracy. Between the two
the literary artist of to-day finds shelter—at least
temporarily—from the cruel blasts of commercialism. Horace himself incurred the censure of
Maecenas, as he frequently records

Mollis inertia cur tantum diffuderit imis oblivionem sensibus
pocula Lethaeos ut si ducentia somnos ardente fauce tra-
   xerim
candide Maecenas, occidis saepe rogando.*

and for reasons which to this day exhaust his patience. But it is not only indolence and wine which
strain the relations of author and patron. Beneath
that charm of family friendship lurk the grim figures on the sales sheets, and when these conspire
with fate, then not all the endearing words and
affectionate moments of the halcyon days can obliterate them. The eternal child discovers that
business is business, after all, and that batiks and
all the paraphernalia of purchasable art cannot
blanket the real passion that smolders in the bosom
of Maecenas up-to-date. He is not in business for
his health. His technique is new, but his aim is
the aim of his forefathers who set more resolutely
to work to provide the means for such experiments
as this. The artist has his choice—with or without
an anesthetic?

* Again I assist those who, not being younger æsthetes, have no
convenient dictionary of quotations:
"Honest Maecenas, you distress me by asking constantly why
soft indolence has infused into my inmost senses an oblivion as
great as though I had drained with parched throat the cups that
bring Lethean sleep."

6. A PRESS AGENT

UNLIKE all other creative artists, the press agent is made, not born. That is to say, he either achieves greatness or has it thrust upon him, being the lucky victim of circumstances over which he has full control. In his purest form he begins with the usual illusions of literary grandeur, but at an early stage he realizes that art is long and life is short, so he proceeds to concentrate upon the latter. Following the advice of Omar Khayyám, he takes the cash of writing and lets the credit of literature go; he does not care who makes the nation's æsthetics provided he writes its advertisements. He is the *Realpolitiker* of journalism, whose realism enables him to appreciate the difference between the underpaid anonymity of the newspaper man and the overpaid anonymity of the publicity expert. If, as is frequently the case, his English is almost illiterate, he knows that there· are greater rewards for turning his mangled syntax and specious vocabulary to the service of Commerce than for adapting the same jargon to the uses of statesmen. When, as occasionally happens, he has a real feeling for words and language, he is glad to become one of that company of inglorious, perhaps, but never mute Miltons, in whose advertising copy the highest flights of American style are sought by connoisseurs of literature.

Even the darkest cynicism hesitates at the thought that the press agent was originally included in Nature's plan.   There are certain truths from which mankind instinctively averts its gaze, in order that the onward and upward march of humanity be not arrested by a too overwhelming consciousness of man's incurable absurdity, and of the presence somewhere in the universe of a cosmic practical joker. We have to preserve, at all costs, our respect for our Darwinian forebears, and thus we avoid comparisons which might force us into an inverted Fundamentalism, with an emphasis upon "The *Descent* of Man" unintended by the still unpopular author of that engaging tome.   Let us, therefore, ignore the facts, as becomes all earnest theorists, let us forget that the universities have now added the arts of publicity and advertising to the humanities of an earlier civilization, and that belles lettres have made way for follow-up letters as the proper study for the rising generation.   Let us think of the press agent as the result of accident rather than design.

He is a phenomenon so essentially of our time that his origins are not lost in the haze of antiquity. Carlyle has suggested that a collection of books is the best university, but it was at a reporter's desk in a newspaper office that the press agent acquired his incomparable knowledge of human nature, the citadel from which he sallied forth to wrestle with the day's emergencies.   The latter were so varied that he soon developed the talents required, a chameleon capacity for coping with a new religion or an ancient evil, a politician making an exhibition of himself or a foreign genius giving an exhibition of his pictures.   The theater and politics naturally attracted him by making fewer demands upon his intelligence than the humaner arts, and it was there that he received his first call to the sacerdotal office which he now adorns. It all began in the theater.

Among the various functions on his paper which he cumulated was that of twenty-fifth assistant dramatic editor. On nights when fifty new plays opened in New York he attended two of them or, more accurately, he "covered" them. Otherwise his relation to the drama consisted in keeping up an extensive visiting list among the various hierarchies of the theatrical profession. By correlating the effect upon his social intercourse of the views expressed by him in his capacity as a critic, he found himself in that state of grace when the soul is prepared for revelation. In short, being a practical man, he discovered that it made things easier in his normal work as news gatherer when, as arbiter of the dramatic elegancies, his attitude was one of mellow indulgence and ready enthusiasm. In self-defense he was driven, at times, to escaping after the first fifteen minutes, sustained by the simple device of a program and a conversation concerning the merits and subsequent developments of the play, usually a conversation in the lobby with some one obviously qualified to impart the information by reason of a personal interest in the fortunes of the production.

After a period of such apprenticeship in the art of pleasing, he was gratified, if not surprised, by an invitation to become the press agent of a leading impresario. His common sense told him that his simulated enthusiasm could be more frankly and adequately rewarded when at the service of one man than of the twenty whose endeavors he invariably greeted with journalistic applause. And so he made his exit from the newspaper world, to which he never returned except as an outside Force, whose offerings of news were received first with the good-natured hospitality to which an old colleague is entitled, and finally, in his apotheosis, with deferential wonder, tempered by the satisfactory thought that this Napoleon of the billboards, this hokum Hannibal, had once been a humble newspaper man. So long as he remained in the relatively embryonic stage of the theatrical press agent, his friends on the press were helpful. He got more pictures into the rotogravure section than many an older colleague, and in one of the most independent and conservative papers succeeded in causing two nudes to appear where none had appeared before. The amount of free space which he managed to pre-empt, by luck or cunning, if collected in one spot, would have created such a vacuum as even nature would not dare to abhor.

Such a strategist naturally did not tarry upon the lower slopes of the Broadway Parnassus. He was soon swept up to the heights by an impresario worthy of such advertising, a veritable Barnum of the beaux arts, whose hypnotic influence seemed capable, for a time, of reducing the American public to a stunned acquiescence in all his enterprises. A season of plays in the original Esthonian enchanted the ears of crowded audiences, including authentic specimens of the Tired Business Man, for once engulfed in the cultural ecstasies of his wife and daughter. At prices in excess of those cheerfully paid for bawdy comedies and the glorification of unclothed American girls, he satisfied an extraordinary appetite for drama that was incomprehensible to thousands who had rejected this fare when presented to them in the more easily digested form of English translation. Critics whose belief in the theater of to-morrow involved a deep contempt for the old-fashioned realism of yesteryear could not restrain their admiration for the art of a theater whose original fame rested precisely upon that outmoded realism of thirty years ago.

The mysteries of Finnish or Esthonian were unfolded by diligent manipulation of the herd mind, wherein the press agent played no small part. He disinterred a forgotten book on the evolution of the drama in the Baltic States, had it appropriately refurbished and issued as a new contribution to learning, on a subject in which none was interested on its first publication but two short years before. The higher vandalism proceeded at such a pace that refined and great artists began to be touted around by methods comparable to those of the circus manager at a country fair, intent upon procuring yokels to visit the bearded lady and the two-headed calf. Grandiose spectacles were staged, from the creation of the world to the crucifixion of Christ; there was no pageant in history which could not be "put over" by this irresistible press agent and his master; the newspapers were filled with stories of kings and queens, peeresses and princesses, all engaged for the same parts by the enterprising impresario. People forgot their Esthonian enthusiasm as they scanned the picture sections for photographs of further celebrities waiving new contracts or complaining of the violation of old agreements. The Middle West was swamped with the forgotten foreign novelties of New York, and world-famous stars littered the way-

side, some even dying in obscure places through
which this victorious caravanserai had passed in its
march from the sea.

There remained but one world to conquer, and
so to the movies the press agent directed the hyp-
notist's attention. Between them they succeeded
in making a colossal success out of an already colos-
sally successful star. They made the première of
a new film seem so important that nobody even
smiled when the press declared that, owing to the
rush of European celebrities wishing to be present,
the number of seats available for mere Americans
would be limited. Analogies were established between the movie and the opera, on the ground that
they had, in this instance, a common theme. It
was obvious, on the same principle, that one should
abandon Shakespeare and hasten to the cinema, because there was no perceptible difference between
them, inasmuch as the titles were written in the
tongue that Shakespeare spake . . . more or less.
The Shah of Persia was engaged, for a consideration
that, as usual, sounded better in publicity notes than
in dollar bills, to act as head usher, and various
pleasant and ingenious schemes were devised to
make the motion picture as exotic as all the previous undertakings had been. The familiar idols of
the plain people were sicklied o'er by the pale cast
of oriental thought. It was a healthy pallor, as
the box office receipts showed.

It was also the beginning of a new phase in the
career of the press agent, whom we shall know
henceforth as a public relations counsel. His vault-
ing ambition o'erleaped the barriers which separate
the world of mere amusement from that of the

rarely amused, the world of commerce and public affairs. He effected the transition through the combined social and professional prestige which his connection with the movies brought him, having met at a party an eminent business man whose soul was not insensible to beauty, when blonde and lively. For a period he served as the head of the firm's publicity department, and for a commensurate salary provided them with advice of which he has furnished specimens in a masterly volume of retrospection and analysis. Thus, when the demand for a commodity fell off, he would point out that it *had* fallen off and insist upon the necessity of discovering why. If, by chance, the demand arose again, he would naturally point with pride to the results, or as he would say "the resultant responses" to his diagnosis, at which, apparently, no firm could arrive without such a "consultant" as he. It was the ease with which he remained employed while proffering assistance of this illuminating character that decided him to set himself up in an independent profession.

He installed the kind of office which is depicted in the advertisements of the "quality group" of popular magazines, to that extent justifying the existence of his own craft. But it was not his intention to waste any more of his abilities on mere advertisement writing. To use his favorite word again, he was now a "consultant," who expected to be called upon in real emergencies. The sort of problem he professes to solve is one by which less ingenuous—or disingenuous—minds are baffled. But he has a technique which, on his own showing and by testimony of his delighted clients, is infallible. Let us assume, for the sake of illustration, that the New York subway is even more crowded than usual, and perhaps some one is trampled to death. The situation presents no terrors for the counsel on public relations. For an adequate fee he will explain that the victim died because there was not enough room in the subway. He will quote some profound work, such as "The Herd Instinct in Peace and War," in proof of the fact that, when crowds get into a panic, politeness disappears and the weakest go under. He will then declare that what the Transit Company must do is to reduce the number of passengers or provide more transportation facilities. The former being easier than the latter, he prepares a chart showing the movement of immigration into America, draws public attention to the openings for labor in Central Australia, and establishes statistical evidence demonstrating that the quota system must necessarily diminish the stream of New York traffic. Having done this, and lodged a check in the bank, he is soon absorbed in some other problem, for clients in search of this wisdom clamor for attention.

The public relations counsel rightly claims that he is more than a press agent, for the press agent, after all, undertakes to secure publicity for something and does it, whereas the counsel on public relations professes to solve insoluble difficulties and doesn't. Equipped with a vocabulary borrowed from the psychologists, he becomes a "psychological engineer," an expert on behaviorism, an authority on "the basic mechanism" of public opinion. He is the medicine man of the industrial tribe, whose spells and incantations work wonders which, like all religious mysteries, are either absurd or incredible when viewed by the rational mind. When the number of bobbed-haired women is increasing daily he is not afraid to claim publicly that he has assisted the waning sales of a hair net company by promoting a campaign against bobbed hair. His stock in trade, apart from his inimitable vocabulary, consists of the amazing seriousness with which he suggests the obvious and convinces himself that, once his suggestions have been followed, the matter is closed. He undertakes to make wars as popular as soap and cigarettes; and he will do for mushroom European governments what he once did for chorus girls—he will "sell" them to the American public; he will "put them over." It is impossible either to burlesque the kind of operations of which he boasts in proof of his sagacity, or to parody the pseudo-scientific language which he talks. In homely parlance it used to be said that a person had not enough wit to come in out of the rain. Nowadays, apparently, these people come in, but not until a public relations counsel has told them that they will get wet if they don't, and has guaranteed them against the recurrence of showers.

In this supreme incarnation the publicity man takes on a somewhat inhuman grandeur, consequent, no doubt, upon the almost divine attributes which he claims for himself. While he dwells in the higher spheres of the "consultant" or conducts disciples through the academic groves of the new learning, where ad writing and sales talk are a substitute for education, the ordinary world of the press agent continues to revolve in its own orbit. The word "press agent" is abhorrent to the superman of the species, and so the career is gradually becoming a further opportunity for the glorification of the American girl.   In this new rôle she is now a familiar figure, and the better her figure the more effective her propaganda for the good, the untrue, and the beautiful.   The sternest editors cannot refuse the friendly coöperation in their dramatic sections of appealing young things, wide-eyed, entreating, who come bearing gifts not altogether Danaän, for their copy is frequently excellent.   To the task of producing enthusiasm at a moment's notice these ladies bring those gifts natural to their sex, which the male can rarely acquire.   They possess, moreover, a feminine faculty of hero worship, combined with a complete emotional detachment, which lends to their utterances the peculiar fervor of the auctioneer when praising a work of art.

Thus by the graceful touch of a woman's hand the business of the honest press agent, who knows nothing of the behaviorists or herd instincts, is redeemed from the mummery with which the public relations counsel endeavors to clothe it.   A woman who undertakes to place a paragraph in the press, a picture in a rotogravure section, or an anecdote in a Sunday supplement, has no need of psychological hocus-pocus.   Like Rousseau on a celebrated occasion, she has looked into her own heart and she knows mankind.   The "resultant response" is never in doubt, unlike the tests of the psychological engineers.   If the rewards of this virtue in actual achievement seem slight in comparison with those received by the counsel on public relations, if they seem unfair, may this not be the clew to the whole mystery of the higher hokum?   The "consultant" is

paid, not for what he professes to do, but for what
he prevents others from doing.   He provides the
propaganda which takes the place of public opinion.
Hence the naïve charm of his childlike narratives
of his own powers.   He is a child playing with toys
while his superiors decide what he shall do.

7. A CRITIC

THE size of his brief case is the measure of his estimate of his own importance. He rarely goes far without this imposing piece of impedimenta, with adjustable locks, heavy straps and an attractive array of compartments, containing manuscripts, review books and volumes deserving a place in every gentleman's library. Lest he be mistaken for a mere journalist, he is careful to encumber himself simultaneously with his bag and his walking-stick. The former alone might denote the presence of a common newspaper man, the latter unaided, might suggest dramatic criticism, whereas our Critic is nothing if not a scholar, and his most casual notice of a book assumes the portentousness of a contribution to learning. Not that he has fitted himself for his career by the attainment of the qualifications necessary for criticism. He learns while he earns, and, like the education of George Moore, his is also conducted in public, but not with such happy effect. He is either engaged in displaying the knowledge which he should have quietly digested in his nonage, or he strenuously exhibits his emancipated indifference even to the rudiments of that elementary learning. His pedantry is as depressing as his callow Philistinism.

The Critic of the strictly up-to-date model manages amazingly to combine these two elements, and it is this amalgam which best symbolizes the type under whose ægis a new era in literature has developed. For his pedantry, his defective college education must be held responsible. At college he must have acquired those undigested slabs of knowledge upon which he now ruminates. Had they been properly assimilated, some sustenance might have gone into his style, and a sounder and riper judgment into his criticism. But he is a species of critical Peter Pan, who never grows out of his tutelage to the pedagogue upon whose verbal or written counsel he relies to the end. The gerund-grinder is presumably so charmed at finding a pupil in whom all interest in literature was not stifled, that he encourages his *protégé* in the ways of the New Solemnity. So the latter becomes publicly a book reviewer but privately nurses the sacred ambition to become a critic.

To this end he proceeds to make up for the lost reading more appropriate to his college days. Dusting off his literary manuals, he discovers the names and works of the august dead, to whom he turned a rather inattentive ear before he realized that the call to criticism had been vouchsafed to him. He determines to make these his companions, and to refresh his soul after the daily trivialities of current book reviewing with those masterpieces which have stood the test of time. If he were on the far side of fifty instead of hovering uncertainly about thirty, he would assuredly say that every time a new book appears, he rereads an old one. As it is, he has his moments, as when he can dismiss conversation about some contemporary by reverting to the sermons of John Donne or to Hobbes's "Leviathan." One gathers that his great consolation is the fact of his being so cultured that, when he has solemnly criti-

cized the inadequacies of "The Sheik" or "Flaming
Youth," he can retreat to the blessed company of
Montaigne and Aristotle. He deprecates the time
wasted upon the contemporary American realists,
and ingenuously urges the superior claims of Fanny
Burney and Mrs. Aphra Behn.

His technique is of the simplest. Being too old
to avow his ignorance and not young enough to
admit his inexperience, he feels compelled to give
constant reminders of his wide reading and cultured tastes. Thus he will begin: "I was looking
through 'A Mirror for Magistrates' last night for
the hundredth time, when I came across a passage . . ."; or "I have just been rereading 'The
Diall of Princes'; it is really far better than 'Mirrors
of Downing Street'"; "Don't you think that Eugene O'Neill is very much less worth while than
Vanbrugh?" He will establish parallels between
Fielding and Sherwood Anderson, to the latter's dis-
advantage, and establish charges of plagiarism
against "Ulysses" by means of quotations from
Jacobean divines. He is charmed when he catches
a friend tripping in some matter which he himself
has picked up second-hand through Professor Saints-
bury or Mr. Charles Whibley. Although he professes the utmost scorn for reprinted critical articles
—until his own are collected—he combines this
with an unbounded admiration for Hazlitt and
Arnold. These have been hallowed by the bene-
diction of the class-room handbooks. Their journalism has now become criticism; his professors have
told him.

His own practice as a critic presents few de-
partures from the norm of mortals who deem them-

selves less gifted. He shows a becoming discretion where the works of editors are concerned, and the elucubrations of his teachers fill him with appropriate humility. When he finds a book of criticism in a field where he has aspired to disport himself, he will conscientiously expose all its weaknesses, if the author happens to be a person of little editorial consequence. He will pronounce judgment upon the excellence of translations, from languages of which he is ignorant, with an air of the profoundest expert knowledge. He regards these utterances with a pontifical earnestness, and believes that his being asked to write a review is an event of considerable importance to the author in particular and to the public in general. Any work of arresting quality excites him to denigration, and his fault-finding is filled with echoes of the platitudes of the type leveled against George Meredith, to the effect that his style was obscure, and that his characters spoke a language never overheard in buses. He is just a little vague in his mind as to this question of realism. He finds that all his professors seem to agree that realistic fiction is reprehensible, but whenever there are no romantic stereotypes, and phonographic reproductions of speech make way for genuine writing, then the poor fellow is distressed and puzzled. In short, in his premature desire for balance and perspective, he generally achieves priggishness.

When the Critic's aim, on the other hand, is to astonish the bourgeoisie, he usually succeeds in giving the educated an astonishing exhibition of his own ignorance, real or assumed. In this phase of his evolution he has simply reversed the order already described. He will not, on any account, ad-

mit that a classic, ancient or modern, is worth reading. To suggest merits in Thackeray is somehow
to detract from the fame of Waldo Frank. The
idea that the full flavor of Ring Lardner is enhanced
by contrast with one's appreciation of Goldsmith
or Bacon, is one which his ultra-modern mind refuses to entertain. The consequence is that the victim of this obsession begins his career as an æsthete
and ends as a reporter, incapable of any judgment
other than "I don't know much about art, but I
know what I like." In his æsthetic stage he is a
source of not altogether innocent merriment; in the
reportorial, he is the most potent force in modern
criticism.

Who can resist the humor of the baubles that be-
dizen the prose of the æsthetic critic, who declares
swooningly: "The breath of a rare aptness informs
every rectangle of canvas or glass decorated by
Marsden Hartley. . . . Like a warm flower half
hidden by lush grasses, the presence glints from his
clamant shields of color, meeting with light reassur-
ance the eye when first it falls upon the great drooping curves, the prim angular shapes and flaunting
areas of this simultaneously stiff and violent and
whimsical art." One is suffused by grammatical
blushes when one reads: "Lyric substance has gotten
a novel acidulousness of him," or "the sharp things
make gay dangerous guerilla upon the alkalis coat-
ing the brain." Another blush is produced by such
obstetrical images as "known in the body of a
woman, the largeness of life greets us in color," or
"what men have always wanted to know, and
women hide, this girl sets forth. Essence of woman-
hood impregnate color and mass." It is more in

joy than in anger that one discovers that these sweet phrases are those of a critic who believes that the great auk is the bird known as the great roc in the "Arabian Nights"—after all the "Arabian Nights" were not written last year at the MacDowell Colony. They don't belong.

When he forsakes these exotic jungles of words, so appropriate to the art with which they purport to be concerned, the Critic is then liable to lapse into the genial or conversational manner, which has a potency that can medicine booksellers and readers to the sweetest of sleeps. Genial, when the arbiter of our literary destinies addresses his readers in general by fanciful names, and his personal friends in the "literary game" by nicknames and affectionate diminutives. We learn what he found in the icebox last night, after an evening's toil, how his dog bit the baby and the Ford ran out of gasoline just outside Jamaica, L. I. . . . . Incidentally, it seems that "dear old Jackie" has written another masterpiece (publisher and price indicated), that he is a hell of a nice fellow and spends five hours at his lunch when his critic is with him. It further transpires that the Critic has just been round the book shops and has picked up a fine copy—in Everyman's Library—of "Typee." He has no hesitation in recommending this hitherto neglected and unknown work to his sweet customers. The customers aforesaid do not wait to be told twice—although, as a matter of arithmetical fact, they hear the same thing twice daily for several weeks after—they rush to the book shops, and "dear old Jackie" shares with Herman Melville a species of boom.

The more intensely personal and domestic the

Critic becomes, the more insistent he is that the
"we" reserved for editorial writers and royalty shall
be his pronoun. Upon which analogy, let the charitable and uncharitable explain according to their
diverse temperaments. It does seem as though an
"I" could hardly strike a jarring note in so intimate a picture, but such egotism is rigorously ex-
cluded. Instead, one gets an obviously detached
account of how "we" were lunching on board the
"Aquitania," when "our" dear old friend Tommie
So-and-So confided that he was publishing a new
book, and, without having seen it, "we" can swear
to its excellence and entreat "our" dearest patrons
to order it at once. At the same time, the same
publisher is bringing out a series of reprints in which
"we" discover a delightful book which "we" had
never read, but which "we" now intend to boost till
many moons and many columns have waxed and
waned. Whereupon a breathless audience is made
aware of the existence of "Robinson Crusoe," "The
Three Musketeers," or some similar obscure volume.
The genial Critic is much beloved of publishers and
booksellers. He is a popular educator. He knows
when to give credit where credit is due. In the
trade they say he has "a large following."

He has an alter ego, however, whose typewriting
on the wall is a more powerful omen than that
which troubled the feast at Belshazzar's court. The
Critic unadorned makes no play with his ice-box,
his lunches, the dog by his fireside and the dawn
coming up like thunder across Oyster Bay. No
poetic pictures in the pseudo-Lamb manner for him,
no references to rare Ben Jonson, cheese and ale.
He is a regular guy, who would as certainly prefer

a ball game or a session at poker to the books which he has to discuss, as would the husbands of all the ladies who read him. When he can, he escapes and entertains the men with his genuine appreciation of all manly sports. But the women want culture, and so he tells them what their menfolk refuse to speak. He can put them on to a good mystery story, another analysis of the problem of sex and, every now and then, a work of more or less serious intent which happens to deal with some question which arouses his natural feeling in favor of fair play. He can "sell" them an idea.

What, however, is vastly more important, he can sell books, and is thereby unanimously constituted the world's greatest Critic. His name adorns the jackets and advertisements of many books, and lucky, indeed, is the publisher who can quote him as saying: "Get me, kid, this sure is some humdinger of a story, holy gee!" When he concludes his examination of some new contribution to the literature of domestic slavery, his peroration brings joy into many a publisher's humble home: "By gosh, this jane has hit the high spots of married life. The best book we have read in years," or words to that effect. Whereupon carloads of paper rumble Eastward, printing presses revolve, in the moving picture market there is a flurry, and the American home is enriched by one more triumph of the native genius.

In criticism he is man as Rousseau desired him, in his natural state, unspoiled by the affectations which bedevil his less fortunate rivals. Fundamentally their equipment is the same, but the others present those fluctuations from the normal which do not add one cubit to their critical stature, but seriously detract from their usefulness as the accurate reflection of mass opinion. Others may stumble occasionally upon a book which proves to be just what the public wants, but they cannot be relied upon to repeat the performance instinctively. The Critic unadorned can arrive by second nature at the judgments expected of him; his reactions are as standardized as Ford parts and as reliable. If he cherishes any secret desires of a subtly intellectual or æsthetic kind, he conceals the stirrings of this libido from the profane gaze. His habit of reiteration sometimes leads to his methods being confused with those of his more introverted colleagues. When he returns again and again to praise of the same book, he is animated by no more reprehensible motive than that which prompts a child to voice its pleasure in repeated singsong. He wants the public to share his enthusiasm.

His naïve rejoicings, in fact, prove now and then his undoing. Rival publishers have hardly passed advertising proofs in which he greets their particular goose as a swan, when each discovers that their respective masterpieces have been hymned in identical terms as "the best we have read." Sinister suggestions are made by the disgruntled, who assert that this appearance of candor covers an elaborate system of log rolling, but the charge cannot be proven. It is irrelevant, moreover, because it lies against every writer who is called upon to pass comment upon current literature. As usual, the individual is blamed for the achievements of the plain people. It is their recognition which confers the power against which those who cannot benefit by it protest. Henry James could not have sold an edition of "The Egoist" by boosting "old Dick Meredith."

There are certain risks which our Critic does not take. If he did, he would not be the phenomenon which he is. If he were even liable to such lapses from normalcy, he could not wield the influence which makes him the complete Critic in our time. He can do none other, Demos helping him. But it is in no spirit of martyrdom that he can adapt those words to fit his case. He is a round peg in a perfectly round hole, unlike the many square pegs which fit so uneasily into the critical places assigned to them in this age of Equal Opportunity. We live, it is said, in a democratic era, and we pay the penalty of our daring. With greatness thrust upon him before he has attained competent mediocrity, the Solemn Critic inevitably plays at being grown-up by donning the clothes of his literary parents. The Æsthetic Critic tries to achieve sophistication before he has acquired knowledge. The results are equally absurd. And so we arrive at the logical conclusion: *vox populi, vox critici.*

Casting his shadow over the whole scene stands the professor, who usually possesses all the qualities which the other simulate, but none of the virtues which make those qualities desirable. He has a certain background and real perspective, but urbanity, intellectual curosity and sensitiveness to new ideas are lacking. He lives in his water-tight literary department, so cut off from the world of contemporary letters that even those whom he pursues in his feuds are phantoms to him. He has the distressing habit of lumping all his dislikes under some generic epithet, and dies unaware that the groups which he has indicted have as little in common amongst themselves as they have with him. His particular phobias are the "younger set" or the "Bohemians," but he has never troubled to find out which writers actually belong to these categories. He can see no difference between an Æsthete: Model 1924, and the antithesis of this phenomenon: Theodore Dreiser and H. L. Mencken. In his rasher moments he confounds Van Wyck Brooks and Burton Rascoe in an identical excommunication. When he rides forth in his literary Klan robes, he runs amok, and insinuates that the brachycephalic Mediterranean, or even the Jewish taint, is present in writers of authentic Dutch lineage dating back at least two hundred years. He calls for the instant deportation of such aliens, when their works displease him, on the ground that they are unassimilated and un-American. The Academic Critic is a species of Fundamentalist in literature.

When he becomes a Modernist the fruits of his condescension are rather dry. He remains the schoolmaster to the end, but develops an extraordinary faculty for balancing on critical tight ropes. His lack of prejudice—ostensible prejudice—becomes positively embarrassing. One watches breathlessly while he trips along the slack wire of his cautious prose, maintaining a skillful balance, so that he can praise with equally discreet enthusiasm exponents of diametrically opposite and irreconcilable tendencies, without once revealing towards which side his own convictions incline. Finally the truth emerges, that he has no convictions outside the accepted figures of the past, where a certain degree of liberty of judgment is permitted to a scholar and a gentleman. He can argue for or against Poe and Whitman—there are academic precedents for whatever side he takes. Otherwise, his indifference enables him to be all things to all new men of letters, but at times his assumed enthusiasm threatens the prerogatives of the journalistic amplifiers. At this precise moment in his evolution he is at his zenith, for he then combines the commercial influence of the regular fellows with the parchment prestige of the pedagogue. His ramifications are many. He is the Great Power in American letters.

8. *A LIBERAL*

H E is one of the strange by-products of Anglo-Saxon civilization, the fine flower of a social order based upon parliamentary government and evangelical Protestantism. As these fundamental elements of his being indicate, compromise is the breath of his nostrils; his very essence is the uncompleted gesture, the half-truth, the safe evasion of harsh facts. His point of departure being those two colossal compromises, representative government as a substitute for revolution, Dissent as a substitute for free thought, his ideas have been vitiated ever since by an inherent dishonesty. His representative government does not represent, and his Protestantism confers no freedom of opinion—both are travesties of the ideals which first inspired them, and they are typical of Liberalism and its works. They are the jewels set in the crown of modern radicalism: both false.

The marrow and quintessence of Liberalism must not be forgotten if we are to arrive at a proper estimate and understanding of the curious biped evolved from that primeval slime of ill-conceived and unrealized ideas. In his strictly contemporary incarnation the Liberal may seem to belie his origins. He is perpetually engaged in a querulous denunciation of the evils of political democracy, and, more often than not, he has discarded the simple Gospel teaching of his parents. But it is characteristic of him that he proposes to improve political democracy by extending its ravages, and into what he doubtless calls his intellectual activities he carries the evangelical unction of the Gospel tent mission and the furtive equivocations and shufflings of Chadband and Pecksniff. Whatever is, is bad, whatever was is worse, whatever will be, must be better. In short, the Liberal believes in progress, while he demonstrates that it is impossible.

Politically the Liberal is almost extinct and completely absurd. When the world war crashed through the glass of the hothouse in which he had drowsed so securely for a generation, when his ideas were dragged out of the padded cells where they had gyrated so harmlessly, he discovered a very wicked world, indeed, which spurned his nostrums because of their obvious futility. With the return of peace he found his occupation gone. Since then he has taken refuge in a lachrymose benevolence, in the hope that this exhibition of the tenderness of his heart will divert attention from the paucity of his ideas. The economic tangle presented by a newly delimitated Europe and the problem of reparations, involving, as they do, a fundamental revaluation of all previous social, industrial and natural values, very naturally dismays the Liberal, who never faced a fundamental idea during the whole course of his existence. Consequently, he turns gladly to the obvious escape provided by the actual misery of the people, and counts with an almost sadistic emphasis the protruding ribs of starving school children. These more accessible totals make a counterplay to juggling with the trillions and quintillions of reparations, reconstruction and depreciated currency.

However deep in the sand of sophistry he buries his head, the Liberal cannot quite evade the specter of his own performances in the years preceding the war and during the apocalyptic years of the conflict. When the social order in which he had trifled so comfortably with brilliant and advanced ideas was engulfed, when the victim's chin was just above the water, he was running up and down the shore, making frantic noises, lapsing into hysterics, and crying out to heaven that he had always besought his dear friend not to go swimming beyond his depth. To those who suggested rescue, he argued as to the exact whereabouts of a certain life-belt which ought to have been in its place but was not. Suddenly he was taken by the scruff of the neck and thrown in, whereupon he swallowed his fears and shouted lustily in praise of aquatic sports, lost in admiration for his own daring. An artificial contraption was thoughtfully provided, in the shape of air-filled propaganda wings, and as he floated with the help of these he began to upbraid such of his obstinate friends as remained ashore. He denied that he had ever declared those seas dangerous, protested his infinite pride in this opportunity to prove his skill and courage, and whenever the waters broke over his head, he rejoiced in the common danger which beset them all. He no longer thought of a danger, but insisted that, so long as the chin was visible, they were actually on dry land.

When the great experience was over the Liberal became suddenly conscious that he had not cut a very brilliant figure. His bathing suit did not fit, he had a perceptible paunch, and his muscular development was of the slightest. He noticed that there was a lamentable tendency to smile on the part of those who had witnessed his being rushed in where his ideals feared to tread, that esteem was reserved only for those who had acted either on impulse or principle, but for the forced acquiescence of such as himself there was only contempt. His prestige was irrecoverable. The very objects of his vast solicitude in the old days proved ungrateful. The vipers nourished in the tepid bosom of Liberal▪ ism bit hard. The oppressed nationalities, whose woes had formerly incited him to such tearful elo▪ quence, turned out to be monsters of imperialism, drilling and arming and taxing, oppressing those in their power in a thoroughly democratic imperialist manner. His poems about the horrors of war are now remembered only by the Liberal literati; the men who fought prefer the lewd epic of "Mademoiselle from Armentières" to the defeatist stanzas of the Liberal warriors. The rendez-vous with death is forgotten in memories of rendez-vous of an all-too-human kind. As for the plain people, whose aims the Liberal insisted upon interpreting, they collapsed safely into the arms of Mussolinis, or, unkindest of all cuts, elected Labor governments with programs indistinguishable from those of Liberalism in its heyday, but unsoiled by the contamination of that ludicrous word.

With a more or less subconscious realization that his political life is ebbing away the Liberal is beginning to turn upon the object of his solicitude an inquiring eye. What, he wonders, can be the explanation for the failure of his Messianic mission? And in due course he produces pseudo-scientific volumes of meditations upon the crowd mind, the manufacture of public opinion, and the behavior of herd instincts. Having utterly failed to impress the masses, the Liberal feels himself to be an expert authority on the ways and means of impressing them. Nobody can excel him in diagnosing the evils of the press, in sketching its vast power for good, in divining the supreme excellence of the mob's tastes and intentions. The reason, therefore, why Liberal papers do not flourish is not because they are ineffective and entirely out of touch with human life, but because the sterling nature of the public is exploited for nefarious purposes by the corrupt capitalist press. Papers which thrive on the incurable delight of the people in scandals, comic strips and pictures of wayward wenches do so contrary to the laws of nature, apparently, for the Liberal knows that the readers really crave for enlightened articles on the theater of to-morrow, fearless reports of coal strikes, and impassioned pleas for Peace, Justice, Liberty, Equality and Fraternity.

As a journalist, however, the Liberal places a curious interpretation of his own upon what ordinary, unregenerate human beings understand by fair play. His censorship is vastly more rigid than any known to the organs of commercialism and corruption which he denounces. His periodicals are almost always tied to some propaganda, and everything that appears in them must be shaped so as not to conflict with the delusions of the editors or the particular panacea advocated by their subsidizers. There is rarely room in the columns of a Liberal editor for controversy involving his own beliefs, but controversy concerning the errors and misdeeds of others is welcomed. Usually a sacrosanct group of

the elect completely monopolizes every avenue of
opinion and the evils of competition are thereby
eliminated. No heresies are allowed to creep in to
disturb the somnolent minds of the fraction of the
public which constitutes the Liberal's audience. If
a rival happens to gain an advantage in the prior,
or simultaneous, publication of an article in some
common field of moral endeavor, in truly Liberal
fashion each pretends that his own publication is
the only one which has had the foresight, courage
and sense of the public welfare to undertake that
particular crusade. For their respective superstitions all cordially despise each other, carrying their
feuds and animosities to a point far exceeding the
worst malefactions of their favorite scapegoat, the
Associated Press.

In his accusations against the world in general
the Liberal wholly uncovers his own methods and
practices. He clamors incessantly for impartial and
honest men in the press and in public affairs, raising
a great lamentation whenever he discovers evidences
of friendship and bias usurping the place of objective judgment, but his own weaknesses in this respect transcend the merely notorious and become
positively ludicrous. Every Liberal is a hero to his
own press valet, and radicalism will cover a great
multitude of sins unpardonable in others. Let a
writer trample upon the holiest superstitions of the
sex-conscious feminists, let him exceed in vituperation of majority opinion the secret dreams of the
most impenitent trust magnate, let his repeated
ideals be those of Prussian militarism and monarchical absolutism, the Liberals will fasten to him like
leeches because, when they awoke from the hypnotic

trance of Wilsonism, they discovered that their new and strange ally had consistently vilified and blasphemed their fallen idol. Observe a female of the species, who refuses to be known by her husband's name, persuading herself and others that "In Defence of Women" is a delightful contribution by H. L. Mencken to the propaganda of woman's emancipation. Here the Liberal lambs lie down with the frankest of wolves in so Biblical a manner that one is moved to tears . . . of mirth.

It is the Liberal's aim, apparently, to be the first to throw not a stone but a bouquet at the woman taken in adultery, provided the affair is turned into literature, and the woman becomes a radical novelist. Be she as far removed from reality as the late Eleanor H. Porter, her æsthetic sins will be forgiven her because of the exemplary irregularity of her private life and the old-fashioned unconventionality of her point of view. When reviewed by a Liberal, the novel of a Liberal, however bad, is never so bad as the novel of a conservative, however good. The fellow-feeling which makes them so wondrous kind to each other reaches its logical climax in the more ardent spirits who develop a positive phobia towards everything in literature that is not "modern." From these comes that most superb of all the tribe's variations, the educationalist, intent upon substituting "science" for the humanities, and magnificently impatient with the classics and with classical education. Hear him inveigh against the time wasted upon the literature of the past, when there are so many "splendid books" being written to-day. One is expected to dismiss the Brontës and Jane Austen, in order to revel once

more in the autobiographical narrative of some earnest *révoltée* against the yoke of Methodism in
Iowa, who comes to New York and realizes the possibilities of synthetic gin and promiscuity in the
neighborhood of Washington Square. One must
abandon the mature and charming hedonism of
Horace for the sophomoric eroticism of some queen
of the Poetry Society of America.

Let us be modern says the Liberal, while the
way to his heaven is paved with half-intentions, for,
needless to say, in his educational theories, as in all
other things, he takes immediate flight from the
full realization of the ideas with which he plays.
When the well-barbered, standardized, practical,
tiled bathroomed, thoroughly sanitated, radio-fed
product of modern education looms up, armed with
diplomas in ad-writing and automobile mechanics,
but unencumbered with any knowledge of the un-
enlightened past, then we hear a tirade about the
goose-step in American education. Once again the
Liberal discovers that the beneficiary of his theories
has no sympathy whatever for his benefactor, that
another Frankenstein has been created to terrify his
creator. The perversity of human nature once more
asserts itself, to remind Liberalism of the existence
of that one fascinating and eternal element in life
which is so resolutely ignored by Liberals. However colossal the demonstration of man's natural
talent for backsliding into the jungle where he belongs, the Liberal succeeds in improving upon the
traditional practice of the Bourbons, for he learns
nothing and forgets everything.

It is a touching spectacle to watch him trying to
piece together his shattered world of 1914 with dip-

lomatic telegrams as sticking plasters. If he can
unearth in archives rendered indiscreet by revolutions evidence showing that in Russia some one telegraphed at 9.06 instead of 9.15 on a certain date,
and that somebody else was fishing in Norway on
a particular day in July, 1914, or bathing in a Baltic
watering place—then he feels that the World War is
explained. When a new régime publishes information solely to discredit the old régime, he fondly
imagines that this is done in the disinterested service
of Truth and Peace, and proceeds to found hopes
on the new order, until the inevitable and never
long-delayed moment when history repeats itself.
The performances of the British Labor government are a source of weekly anguish, because of
the punctiliousness with which Mr. Ramsay Mac-
Donald follows the precedents of all statesmen before him, talking to the Mexicans as though he
were a Lord Curzon, and adding to the naval estimates with the Britannic enthusiasm of a Winston
Churchill or Lord Fisher. Owing to the unkind
facts of time and space the telegraphed news of
these imperial gestures frequently coincides with the
hebdomadal horoscopy of some wild-eyed prophet
of the Liberal millennium who announces that the
stars are at last propitious to the dawn of a new era.

His brighter and better day is always just about
to break, and the auspices are as regularly incredible
to any intelligence less resolutely closed to the les-
sons of actual life and experience. In his fact-proof
shelter the Liberal can live through the fiercest as-
sault unscathed. He can go through a war believing that the date of a telegram determined the conflict, and that the horrors of battle have only to be

realized in order to make war impossible. The collective animosities and racial antagonisms of different peoples may flare up every hour of the day even amongst troupes that are Allies, but he imagines that nations would love and understand each other, if it were not for the incitements of wicked capitalists, themselves perhaps the only genuine internationalists in the world. His own publications, periodical and otherwise, demonstrate to an ordinary bookkeeper that the public does not want that kind of reading matter, but he is certain that, if Marx or Thorstein Veblen were substituted for the memoirs of Count Boni de Castellane, the editors who now perversely prefer the latter would double their circulation. When a radical newspaper is launched on its brief career, its readers are not the toiling masses, who never forswear their allegiance to the capitalist paper which sells two million copies daily. It is read by well-to-do Liberals, who finally write the obituary in which it is regularly stated that the failure of this organ of liberty is a grievous loss to the working classes.

The Liberal is the pathetic victim of a fetich known as the People, an abstraction situated outside of time and space, and having no connection with the people whom people know and see. In the cult of this strange and exacting deity, this mythical monster, the Liberal develops into the paradoxical creature familiar to all of us, the man whose personal gloom and melancholy, whose dissatisfaction and discontent are counterbalanced by a limitless theoretical optimism; a person whose sentimental passion for freedom makes him the most intolerant and biased commentator upon life, for he is the

slave of a propaganda whose ends everything must
serve; a champion of all hopeless causes, because
if any of them could be realized he would be frightened and horrified, as is proven whenever political
realists actually set to work upon his assumptions.
In the eighteenth century the French Revolution
induced in him a revulsion of feeling which had
its counterpart in our own time when Tsardom was
destroyed. It would have been so nice if the thing
could have been done by passing resolutions in New
York and London.

It is little wonder that the Liberal is querulous
and narrow, that prevarication, evasion and compromise are the arts at which he excels, for he alone
of all men can never be honest with himself. He
must deal obliquely with situations that cannot the-
oretically arise, but which he must face every day.
He must think in terms of half-measures, for he
can follow nothing to its logical end. Ruthlessness
and cynicism, the saving graces of his adversaries,
are refuges to which he cannot resort. He must
be unfair for the noblest motives, since he cannot
admit his real motive, which is always the usual
human one, material necessity, vanity or sheer prejudice. He never hesitates to make two bites of
a cherry, for his policy is to nibble at it furtively
a dozen times, and then declare that the fruit is
intact. If he were not in a minority, he would have
no means of existence, since it is his function to
talk while other people act, either in defiance of,
or in obedience to, his theories. In both cases he
is dismayed by positive results, for in neither is there
any place for such as he. In the last analysis he
probably prefers to be flouted by his avowed enemies

rather than shamed by his logical friends. The former enable him to go on talking, whereas the latter produce results which reduce him to silence. The emotions of a reformer's to-morrow are so much more soothing than the revolutionary *Katzenjammer* of the morning after the night before.

9. PURITAN: MODERN STYLE

HIS lineage is so ancient that his family has given famous types to every literature, and when hard pressed in argument he tries to shelter behind ancestors who have left records of more than their unpleasant qualities, which are the only traits shared in common with them by their descendants in America to-day. The contemporary Puritan has so far degenerated from his forbears that he can rather quaintly make claims for them, which, by comparison, confer upon them the human characteristics of almost civilized men. It is positively pathetic to watch the attempts to befog the issue made by those who point with pride to the amount of alcohol consumed by the New Englanders of the heroic age in answer to the charge that Puritanism is responsible for the reformist ills that afflict us. While he is conspiring against freedom of thought, freedom of art and personal liberty, the modern Puritan likes to dwell upon the famous Puritans of other days, who wrote and struggled and fought on behalf of some of the very principles which he ceaselessly tries to annul and destroy.

With Mr. William H. Anderson in jail for forgery, it requires something more than an effort of the imagination to correlate the ambitions of that typical guardian of our moral welfare with those of the early martyrs of Puritanism who, if they went to prison, did so on behalf of some principle, in which they, at least, believed without material profit to themselves. An equal capacity for self-deception is necessary to see the connection between an Anthony Comstock and his successors and the Puritanism which inspired a Milton to write his "Areopagitica," to mention another Puritan who was also interested in morals and literature. This ancestry is obviously too distinguished for those who invoke it nowadays to cover up the peculiar practices of the self-appointed latter-day saints. Even a Cromwell, indulging in the sport of baiting Irish Papists, presents certain ordinary, human traits, which one cannot associate with the kind of man who comes whispering into a bookseller's back room, departs triumphantly with a copy of "The Decameron," and then has the vendor arrested or fined for selling obscene literature. For this superb product of Christian endeavor a less honorable parentage must be sought than that which his champions bestow upon him.

The pathological Puritan of to-day is a particular phenomenon, to be studied in relation to the circumstances which have produced him, and without reference to the historical word-quibbling so dear to the hearts of the professors who make a specialty of his defense, as though some precious boon to our civilization would be lost, were he to receive the full discredit which is his due. He is no longer the man who kindles such a flame as will not be extinguished; nor does he suffer for any principle, nor enlist in any cause that might conceivably be of importance to human welfare. He does not even perform efficiently the duties which he assigns to himself and for which he is paid. His goal is steadily receding, and the very abuses which are his stock-in-trade flourish exceedingly, providing a rich record of statistics for the reports with which he annually hypnotizes his dupes. In latent form he is the passive member or supporter of the innumerable leagues and societies of busybodies who have nominated themselves for the task of usurping the natural functions of the law and its officers in civilized states. In his active form he is the paid employee of these people, the professional moralist, whose interest and advantage it is to stimulate the kind of offense in which his patrons are interested, and to extend whenever possible the scope of their interference in other people's business.

The modern Puritan is a horrid mongrel, produced by crossing evangelical fanaticism with democratic paternalism, both nourished on the envy and hatred of the mob for what it cannot understand. In his childhood the candidate for these unholy orders already shows the aptitudes of his calling. He is the boy who curries favor with his teachers by spying upon the doings of his comrades and reporting them. He is the surreptitiously nasty youth who is too pure to share openly in the healthy, animal play of his schoolmates, but who may be found sneaking around corners alone, in search of forbidden sights; who likes bullying little girls, but is too Christian and gentle to face a boy his own match. His highest flight of daring is to lead others into some scrape and then escape himself, leaving them to extricate themselves and take whatever punishment is involved. In brief, at this age he appears, to every one but his doting parents, an arrant little sneak and prig.

His natural evolution brings him together in later life with inferior, intimidated souls of his own kidney, and they generally agree that something must be done to restrain people from leading happier and fuller lives than themselves. They notice that their narrow fears do not seem to penetrate into certain departments of life, which are, roughly speaking, those connected in some way with literature and the arts. To the harassing of this world the Puritan especially bends his efforts. Scandals in politics and commercial dishonesty do not often call forth his fulminations, for he does not conceive of the people concerned as having a particularly good time. Pleasure is the enemy, not evil, and so the joys of mind and body are under suspicion. Evidently joy shall be in the professional moralists' heaven over one publisher who is fined, more than over ninety-and-nine unjust politicians which heed no indictment. All that remains of the traditional stern virtue of Puritanism is a jealousy of everything which offers in this world the consolations advertised as belonging exclusively to the next. Graft and forgery are venial weaknesses, which actually arouse the prayerful to chivalrous defense, but a girl who reads a description of a woman's body by Théophile Gautier is guilty of wickedness deserving the punishment of hell fire.

The pathological state of Puritan morality is constantly demonstrated by the distorted restriction of the term to sexual matters, and the consequent concentration of attention upon all manifestations of the sexual instinct. Artistic creation being essentially an expression of that instinct, the Puritan attacks the root as well as all the branches, and every leaf on the tree of knowledge. Morals, not art, is his concern, and by morals he means perhaps the most fluctuating and elusive part of the whole code of modern civilization. At the very outset of his own Scriptures, murder is established as a crime, but nowhere at any period is obscenity defined. Children indeed, whose minds are in the stage of development at which a vice crusader's must remain, find lewd and lascivious passages in the Holy Bible itself.

Æsthetically, then, the Puritan is a minor, at best. At his worst, he is in literature and art what the grinning yokel becomes when he enters a museum for the first time and sees nude statuary. From the point of view of an uneducated peasant, it is unanswerably true that the Venus de Milo is no less an improper spectacle than any woman of his acquaintance would be, were she to appear before casual strangers in the same unadorned attitude. On behalf of the most undeveloped elements in the community, the Puritan protests, but too often his protests are heeded on precisely the opposite grounds. He tries to infect the rest of us with his prurience, and when he fails, he declares that we are shameless. He has been called a "snouter" with the happiest aptness, for he discovers obscenity as a hog finds truffles, and there are many who savour the delicacies dug out by his probing snout. He is the greatest salesman of pornography, for he has turned into scandalous successes books which had previously enjoyed the quiet appreciation of a limited public.

The psycho-analysts assert that our dreams have a manifest and a latent content, and that by the interpretation of the symbols in which the latter is disguised one may ascertain the psychic trauma from which the patient suffers. What is the latent content of the dream whose manifest expression is the professional Puritan? He is not only indifferent to morality in its broadest sense, but on occasion defends offenses which the law of the land punishes with imprisonment. Morals, therefore, is a mere subterfuge to mask his real aim. He forms no associations of private inquisitors to pursue the innumerable violators of all the most important laws on the statute book. The legislatures all provide for the punishment of offenses against morals as for offenses against life and property. The Puritan does not lead any supplementary body nominated by its own members to ensure the strictest enforcement of the laws against theft and murder. These crimes become increasingly daring; they present a problem in which the authorities might welcome volunteer assistance of an effective kind. But there is no New York Society for the Suppression of Hold-ups, no Watch and Ward Society, intent upon watching for burglars and warding off the attacks of thugs. Physical courage, as we know, was never a strong point with the up-to-date Puritan.

He looks after the crimes which he himself defines in advance, when it is certain that no physical risk is involved. He likes the misdemeanors which are such a menace to the innocent public, that he has to set traps for the culprits· in order to catch them in crime. He has the technique of those who sell gold bricks, for he has to arrange his exhibit in advance so that the properly constituted authorities may be confronted with evidence. The safe-

guards which the community provides for itself are
not good enough for him. He knows that, without his coöperation, we should be helpless to protect ourselves from obscenity at every street corner
and in every book shop. How we ever came to de-
vise legislation against obscenity and blasphemy, it
is hard to say, for it is established beyond the
shadow of a Puritan's doubt that we are utterly de-
bauched, shameless and insensitive to the elementary decencies. If we had our way, John Cleland
and Aretino would be our staple literary fare; our
farces would never content themselves with a harmless naughtiness, but would become unspeakably
filthy; while there would be so much of the American girl to be glorified that the costumers would go
out of business. Nevertheless, we leave all these
things undone, and make it exceedingly difficult for
any of them to be done in defiance of the moral
sense of the community as a whole.

Here we come upon the latent content of the
Puritan dream. He credits us with his own intentions. In his professional capacity he has acquired
a taste for the "Ragionamenti" of Aretino, for
Cleland's "Fanny Hill," for the suggestive passages in contemporary literature. He has a monopoly of procuring them and a talent for discovering
what he is looking for in easily available books,
which has surprised even their authors. He would
hate to see everybody as deeply immersed in such
works as he is. His attitude towards the nude is
such that you cannot persuade him of any difference
between himself and normal, mature men and
women. He knows how much more uncovered he
would like the show girl to be, by his terror of the

effects of what is now permitted. He has his reasons for insisting that women should cover up their arms and necks, and wear the longest skirts into which they can be frightened. They may not be *our* reasons, but how can we prove this? What is bad enough for him is bad enough for us. And so he tries to prevent us from reading "Jurgen," and declares that a man who sells rare lithographs by Rops and expensive limited editions of the erotic classics is imperiling the morals of innocent children, who have neither the knowledge nor the money to obtain these things.

Frustration is the essence of his being, and such pleasures as he has, or can imagine, come largely from the knowledge of the evasion required to attain his purpose. This blessing the Puritan wishes to share with us all, and so he sets out to frustrate our obvious inclinations. These inclinations are not, as a rule, unspeakable, and when they are, we have long since provided safeguards against our own weaknesses. They are the normal inclinations of people who have reached that point in their evolution where they are not insensible to beauty, where they are astride of their own instincts and understand the meaning of morality. These alone are the victims of the Puritan; they alone are hampered and insulted by his incursions into the realms of art, and his attempts to tar them with his own brush in the field of conduct. If he had not the mob behind him, he would be as ready to leave art and morals to the protection of the authorized representatives of the law as he now leaves murder and robbery. But he is the representative man of the botched and intimidated herd, and so he is provided with funds, committees and spies to carry on his moral table-turning and spook-hunting. He can produce the incandescent glow which is mistaken for the flare from the pit of iniquity, and the evil spirit-writing which is regarded by his patron spinsters, without distinction of sex, as the herald of imminent destruction, of the doom of Sodom and Gomorrah.

Obscene, in its original Latin sense, the Puritan is. He is a phenomenon of evil augury to the civilized minority, a reminder of things past, which he does not wish to be forgotten, but which have been left behind. He is the sexual child, but armed with powers which enable him to gratify his infantilism at the expense of mature people. He is haunted by his own morbid imaginings and creates the same disturbance as the obsession of any insane person will amongst the sane. The phantoms which he pursues elude him, of course, because they have no objective existence and can never be reached. If he were not satisfied by the Sadistic pleasure of the actual business of harrying the defenseless, of continually dabbling in matters which by his own confession are harmful, of playing the perpetual Peeping Tom where the maximum thrill to himself is assured—if these things did not absorb his energies, he might realize the futility of his pretensions and the nugatory results which his crusades have achieved.

While he is counting the number of smutty postcards which he seized—by the simple process of answering an advertisement which offered them for sale—and telling his shareholders what return they got on their money, let us see what the up-to-date

Puritan, with an expense account, salary commissions and perquisites has accomplished. Of the "traps for the young" set out in Anthony Comstock's engaging tome with that title, dancing, cards, alcohol, music, painting, sculpture, literature and the theater, every one shows an advance in the contrary direction to that which was his goal. The dances of to-day have moved decidedly beyond the theory that the polka was rather *risquée*, and the waltz the sinuous coil of the Serpent himself. Music as the Puritan commonly understands it—for Tolstoy alone discovered the inward and colossal immorality of great music—has certainly not taken on a demure and spiritual quality, as it is served after supper or during tea at the most fashionable and well-behaved places. Cards are still played and alcohol has merely trebled its "kick" and sextupled its consumption, although the Eighteenth Amendment is the nearest approach to a victory for organized Puritanism, and that only because other forces were finally caught in the stampede. The few books suppressed are now on every young girl's five-foot shelf, while the commonplaces of works which pass unnoticed would have been the occasion of the wildest indignation a few years ago. Pictures of children without their clothes on no longer excite lewd and lascivious thoughts in us, thanks, no doubt, to our uninterrupted contemplation of "September Morn," which marks the date when the Puritan declared that we were all the satyrs of the most pathological kind. In the theater, we have evolved so peacefully that this picture, with a less juvenile heroine, would hardly bring us in any earlier than our accustomed forty-five minutes late nor prevent us from being halfway up the aisle ten minutes before the curtain falls.

Commercialized vice, it would seem, has made way for commercialized purity, for this we have still with us, the last stand of the Puritan. He is now engaged in trying to "sell" us his morality as others sell us tires or cigarettes. But in this business the customer is never right; he must be set right, and a staff of inexpert salesmen attends to the wants that are supposed to be ours. They have an unattractive line of goods, shoddy, shop-soiled, out of date. The Puritan does better in the rural districts, where his wares have, at least, the charm of those hawked by all itinerant bores, whose arrival helps to break the monotony of the isolated. For the intellectually isolated, he provides excitement; he has the glamour of one engaged in hazardous and daring enterprises. In confidence his stories of his experiences bring the thrill of vicarious sin into the hearts of the elect. Perhaps the old and favored clients receive an occasional bonus, in the shape of some wicked trophy from the hunter's collection. Where, if I may adapt Villon, are the obscenities of yesteryear, the loot of last week's raids? As well assume that water can run up hill as believe that these objects so sedulously unearthed are consigned to oblivion. Does a Prohibition Enforcement officer waste the spoils of his office? People don't do such things, as Judge Brack would say. With Omar, I often wonder what the Revenuers buy one half so precious as the stuff they sell.

Thus we find the Puritan of to-day. A hardworking professional, an executive with a staff of well-trained ferrets to carry out his orders, and a board of Tired Business Men, tired by the effort of keeping their noses poked into other people's business. He holds a job and fulfills a function, for he furnishes an excuse for sitting in conference, thereby bringing his methods up to modern standards of commercial efficiency. He incarnates another aspect of the crowd's craving for paternalism, for the presence of some one who will give orders and tell everybody what to do. The Puritan undertakes to do this, and he does it. But his orders are ignored by the very people at whom they are primarily directed. His word is as bad as his law, in the sense that neither has any authority but his own. His preachments are heard only by the converted. He has tried to enter assembly of the arts and, like another Cromwell, to cry "take away that bauble!" The bauble is not so tangible a symbol of authority as the mace which excited the Ironside. He cannot have it removed, for the bauble is that impalpable and elusive and eternal phenomenon, Beauty, in all its manifold manifestations.

10. DOLICHOCEPHALIC

HE is the quintessential American: Nordic, Protestant and white, with Madison Grant and Lothrop Stoddard as his prophets. Through them he became aware of his own identity, for they gave an air of scientific verisimilitude to his otherwise quite convincing narrative of his own superiority, which, in the last analysis, was nothing other than the superiority of the early bird. He regards himself as part of that first flock which migrated to these shores when the worms had not even begun to show themselves in the lush grasses of this vast untilled field, and naturally, when the worms did emerge, they were caught in plentiful numbers by the early birds. But, in the course of time, strange fowl arrived, with hearty appetites, sharp beaks, and an unprecedented talent for grubbing out worms. The promise of American life seemed to be threatened, in a measure, to be unfulfilled, and it became necessary for the elders of the species to draw together for mutual aid, counsel and consolation.

So far as the actual worms are concerned, the dolichocephalics quickly realized that there was little they could do beyond hoarding desperately those already captured. The circumstances demanded highly predatory instincts, even talons, so fierce became the pecking, and wisdom suggested concentration on higher things. Counsel and consolation, rather than mutual aid, were the business

of these councils of the mighty. In the development
of these there evolved the dolichocephalic of to-day,
who has renounced material competition with the
lesser breeds, but has added unto himself all those
things which he has decided shall be the special prerogative of his species. His first concern is the
preservation of the Great Race to which he belongs,
and this is his bulwark, his main line of defense,
his citadel, his strong right arm; with this weapon
he strikes his shrewdest blows and achieves such
victories as are still within his reach. When culprits
are haled before this racial tribunal, he is judge,
jury and prosecutor in the process of deciding
whether there is evidence of brachycephalic mal-
feasance. In his social life this test is a simplifica-
tion, for it provides a plausible reason for the very
human desire to keep away from people whom one
does not like. The victims ponder bitterly upon
their exclusion and never guess that it can spring
from so natural a motive. The dolichocephalic does
nothing to enlighten them. On the contrary, he has
the courage of his evictions, pleading every reason
except the inalienable right of all persons to choose
their own friends.

In a pure dolichocephalic democracy all Nordics
are equal, and the type is at its best when undis-
turbed by the threat of miscegenation. Penetrate
into those retreats which they reserve for themselves,
and you will observe an American scene such as no
casual traveler's eye has ever beheld or pen described. Perhaps one has journeyed through the
hurrying throngs of Lower Fifth Avenue, or even
passed unscathed through the packed subway and
the labyrinthine ways of Grand Central Station, to

reach this nest of gentlefolk. Instinctively one lowers one's voice and removes one's hat on crossing the threshold, for in the very hall there is an air of other-worldliness. No garish cuspidors affright the sensitive gaze, no loud voices shout over the rim of Arrow collars, and deferential servants seem happy to be ordered by gentlemen who know their place. This is a sanctuary, in which the last remnant of an American civilization has taken refuge. It is difficult to believe that this place and its frequenters co-exist with the social order which one has left outside. There are veterans here of wars and struggles upon whose like America will look no more, and whose significance is already as incomprehensible as the Declaration of Independence.

Here, too, is variety of clothes, speech and manner, as befits men who belong to an age whose innocence included, amongst other things, the "consultant" who helps manufacturers to create standardized customers for standardized goods. These irregular fellows do not shave the Mennen way; they do not absorb the shocks that tire them out; they have never run a mile for a Camel, nor smashed a straw hat worn during the hot, sunny days of late September. They seem extraordinarily like the inhabitants of those old countries where one wears a straw hat when the sun compels it; not because it is the 15th of May; where the cut of one's waistcoat and trousers is left to personal taste; where one's barber does not dictate a clean-shaven face, because "everybody is wearing them." It is clearly the democratic privilege of the dolichocephalic to please himself in matters that concern himself alone.

All these men were born equal, but not alike, and so they contrive to look different, to be distinguishable from one another without tags and without those name-plates which symbolically facilitate social intercourse with the conductors of Fifth Avenue buses. One may have come here to mock, but one remains to pray.

The library is a hallowed spot, haunted by the ghosts of the now mythical 'Seventies, lined with books which lack the flamboyant interiors and exteriors of the new dispensation. These books are not the standard by which other books are measured; they are not devastating; they tell no tales of the Jazz Age. They are sober, solid, provincial rather, and sometimes dull. Unless when the raucous voices of his standard-bearers are raised in war cries, the dolichocephalic has no ears for what is loud. He carries on his life on a conversational level, in small type rather than headlines. One suspects that for him alone are the editorial pages of American newspapers written. Their discretion, contrasting with the incautious shouts of the news columns, matches his own. He is the sort of person who would go so far as to divorce his wife, or be unfaithful to her, without writing a best-seller about it.

Amongst his associates there is a notable absence of the names, obliquely reminiscent of the cedars of Lebanon, or directly reeking of turf smoke, evoking the cooling brews of Munich or the garlic plains of Piedmont, which make the telephone directory a microcosm of an un-Kukluxed world. Ex-Europeans have made way for authentic Americans in such oases as those which shelter the dolichocephalic from the boiling heat of the melting-pot. Within his quota not many are called and fewer still are chosen, for he realizes that his high estate is as much a state of mind as a racial distinction. Evidence arguing that head measurements and pigmentation are the tests defeats its own purpose by its ultimate conclusions, for has it not now been proved that the true Nordics in America are negroes? Protestant and blonde, too, are deceptive terms, for when the Nietzschean blonde beasts swept down like wolves upon the democratic fold, a whole area of dolichocephalism was blotted off the ethnic map. The rising tide of color was only the first of the great plagues. His mind is now beset by other morbid fears and superstitions, and to these may be traced most of the phenomena which his enemies rejoice in regarding as the sure and certain signs of his defeat and downfall.

The statisticians have terrorized him with proofs of his comparative infecundity, so that every time he enters the Century Club or the Union League, he has visions of a membership list consisting entirely of such names as Gorgias Xenopoulos, Pietro Golfanello and Moe Tchaftchovitch, when the cataclysm shall have overwhelmed this Republic. He already sees Mediterranean blood on the moon, and dreadful portents are visible to his discerning eye—the shadows which coming events have cast before them. The arts and literature, from the raw material to the finished product—to lapse into the lingo of the interlopers—seem to him to have become the prey of his enemies, who no longer content themselves with the purely commercial fields abandoned to them. From their ranks rise strange authors, musicians and painters; and editors, publishers and

critics to act as retailers, wholesalers and middle-
men, in the most nefarious trade known to the Christian church since opium and white-slavery. Here
is the source of the literature which his daughter
will not let him read, which his club librarian will
not supply, which he has to borrow from the children's rooms some night when they are detained at
"The Nest" or elsewhere, by the music which he
cannot stand and by the liquor which he cannot
drink.

The books are signed by poets and novelists of
dubious dolichocephalism, who either flaunt their
alien syllables on the title-page, or reveal their
character by the expression of opinions which prove
either degeneracy or deception, according as the signature is a genuine or an acquired characteristic.
The canvases and sculpture reproduced in the exotic
magazines to which his club does not subscribe,
strike him as oscillating between the insane and the
bawdy. But all of these creative efforts are saluted
with respect and enthusiasm by a horde of new-
comers, whose vociferations, book jackets, bindings
and advertisements combine in the loudest ca-
cophony. The idols of his childhood are forgotten;
his youngest daughter read "Ulysses" at an age
when her mother was supposed, at least, to be immersed in the polite pages of Augusta Evans Wilson
and Florence Montgomery. The lions of his youth,
Hawthorne and Oliver Wendell Holmes, are the
objects of derision; the companions of his maturity,
H. C. Bunner, George Washington Cable and William Dean Howells, merely produce shrugs of incredulity. Poe and Whitman serve to taunt him
with his shortcomings, and only in the cult of Her-

man Melville is there the inexplicable gleam of a common hope.

The World War stampeded him and completed his disorientation. For a brief moment he regarded the situation, not objectively perhaps, but rationally; with memories of another (to his mind) comparable conflict to steady his nerves. But his totem poles were paraded before him, his ancestral deities were invoked, and soon he was involved just far enough to enable his simian counterparts to take matters into their own hands and do their damnedest. Anglo-Saxons with the most unconvincing patronymics, deodorized and suddenly dehyphenated aliens, snatched the dolichocephalic banner from his amazed grasp, and were soon engaged in practices which, to this day, he will not believe, convinced that the reports of them are subtle Teutonic propaganda. When the available members of his family returned from France, they could not share his paroxysms, nor could he quite understand the detached and disillusioned attitude of the repatriated soldiers of his own breed. The kind of thing he expected came from quarters whither he had never anticipated that he would turn for anything. Misfortune gave him strange bed-fellows, who have arranged ever since to use him as a convenience. He had not even profited by the peculiar opportunities of patriotic service. As he has since discovered, his friends did.

Just as in the housekeeper's room there is duplication of the manners upstairs among the gentry, so in the dolichocephalic mob there is an aping of one's betters. One hears their masters' voices through the brassy distortion of an amplifier. The conservatism, the racial and social pride, are manifested in a violent and brutal form. Exclusiveness degenerates into hunting the foreign-devil; individualism is transformed into herd aggressiveness; racial integrity becomes barbarous tribal fetichism. Masses of inferior men essay collectively to impose ideas and beliefs which can command respect only in one superior man. The American Spartan has allowed his helots to become drunk on the dregs of his own wine. It is an unpremeditated act and will not have the effect upon his children which the deliberate act of the Greeks was designed to achieve. In Dante's hell there was a place for that Pope who had made the great refusal, and metaphorically a similar punishment is meted out in this country for the great abdication.

The dolichocephalic has abdicated. He has surrendered so many things out of inertia and a too easy contentment, that what he holds most dearly is going beyond his grasp in turn. His name is taken in vain, but he makes no protest; his protestations are reserved for matters of less importance. While he re-reads Emerson, and anxiously shudders at the visions of the prophets who foretell his racial extinction, he does not know that his intellectual destruction must precede all other forms of death. Once his spirit has decayed it matters little that he physically exists. Indolence in material things destroyed the aristocratic civilization of the South. A like indolence in intellectual things may have the same result in the case of the Nordic civilization in America. It is characteristic that in the South, where one bulwark against the mob went under, the second is in a perceptibly shaky condition, and the degeneration of the dolichocephalic ideal touches its lowest and most fatuous point. Ku Kluxing is a poor substitute for racial superiority.

In his natural state this Nordic blonde American is a charming spectacle. If he did not exist, some one would have to invent him, in order to make America intelligible to the enlightened foreigner. The cowed, acquiescent, uniform public of the Rotarian Robot régime is clearly not the material out of which American Revolutions are made, nor is it conceivable that a Henry Adams would care to have more than a nodding acquaintance with a Harry S. Daugherty. The authentic dolichocephalic is the last link with an America which had a quality as peculiarly its own as the new America will have when, as seems likely, the old allegiance is shaken off completely. But it was a superior quality. The remains of the old virtues are visible still. Even where orthodoxy is excessive, there is not that rabid, active intolerance which achieves bestiality in some of its current manifestations. There is a deep love of country, but it does not descend to the mechanical goose-step, drill-sergeant level of the popular patrioteers, who want compulsory saluting of the flag, such abject flag fetichism as no intelligent human being can honestly feel.

It is in these respects that the elusive American, whom one so rarely encounters, distinguishes himself from the horde of ex-Europeans, whose special function it seems to be to render ridiculous and obnoxious the very name of Americanism. As one contemplates the harmless dolichocephalic, the man higher up, as it were, it is hard to believe that this benevolent creature can have any connection with the enterprises in which his authority is invoked. If he does not want to lead himself, why does he not dissociate himself from the nonsense identified with his name? As well ask why that name does not figure, with those of Luigi Gozzani, Ivan Kovalevsky, and Isaac Baumblatt, in the list of patriotic, 100% Americans arrested for smashing straw hats each 15th of September. Nobody named Cabot will do the work of an Ole Hansen in Seattle, on the same principle as it is a General O'Dwyer, not Jones or Robinson or Cholmondeley, who shoots down the natives of Amritsar in the defense of England.

What is his connection with the occurrences through which European immigrants and ex-Europeans of recent standing delight to express their devotion to the Stars and Stripes? Can it be that the dolichocephalic believes that this red-blooded Americanism is good for the masses, as certain æsthetic Catholics in France advocate religion for the lower classes, while remaining themselves confirmed atheists? Does he hold that it does not matter who forces the plain people into millions of the same suits and the same hats, induces them to wear their hair in the same way, and smoke the same cigarettes, provided he can order his clothes from London and import his pipes and tobaccos? If this were completely true, one might greet him as a man of genuine skill in the art of living. But it is not exactly the case. It is true only within very distinct limits. He does not practice what his spokesmen preach, that is, he does not subscribe unreservedly to the dogmas of the dolichocephalic necromancers; he makes mental reservations. But, on the whole, he is the victim of his own sooth-sayers.

He has not the complete freedom of an aristo-crat, for he can be persuaded by his inferiors that he has a position to which he must live up, a posi-tion defined by them, instead of one with which they must reconcile their superstitions as best they can. He feels obscurely that he is in honor bound to stand by these crude but energetic people who, they assure him, can save his life. At times he re-minds one of the fable once current about the late lamented Tsar of Russia, a man of excellent inten-tions, it seemed, but entirely out of touch with the common life of his people and surrounded by de-signing favorites. If that is the case of our dolicho-cephalic, then this melancholy analogy needs no apology, for it is prophetic. To the degree in which he himself is the victim of his own servants, he establishes an alibi as to his possible Machiavel-lianism, but, at the same time, he gives us a glimpse of a new horror. He is infected with the herd weakness for uniformity; he has its tendency to acquiesce. His children conform in outward mat-ters even more than he, but they coquet hopefully with the devils that bemuse him, and may end by absorbing and dominating them. When he becomes wholly cowed, and when they, being on the way to standardization, lapse back into his aboriginal aloof-ness from the world as it now is, then, as the French say, we may draw away the ladder.

11. AN APOSTLE TO THE HEATHEN

IN the high and far-off days of splendid isolation he would have been merely incredulous if it had been suggested that America would ever open a lucrative career for his talents. He had then just come down from Oxford and was hardly aware that the North American colonies existed. Fabian socialism was his creed, more or less, but he was an aristocratic radical and had shunned the plebeian society of such Rhodes scholars as might have too sharply reminded him of the overseas dominions. On his arrival in London he had inevitably been caught up in the orbit of those now dimmed stars, then blazing comets of post-Victorian radicalism, for whom what is now euphemistically known as the British commonwealth was simply imperialistic propaganda designed to further the tariff schemes of Joseph Chamberlain. Clean-limbed Englishman though he was, the battles which he won on the playing-fields of Eton were not of the kind that give promise of Waterloos. England, he used to say, was good enough for him, and it was his ambition to be accounted one of the gallant band of Liberal warriors of peace who wished to restore that demi-paradise to its once high estate by means of Fabian social reform. With Wells and Shaw as a pillar of fire in the night of industrialism he came to London to place his pen, his perfect manners and his classical education at the service, not of the People, for he despised them, but at the service of a vague monster whom the early Fabians had christened Social Democracy.

To see him on the lecture platform, or lunching at a women's club in his morning-coat and well-creased trousers of Bond Street elegance, his wing-collar catching the light on its all-British gloss, was a sartorial reminder of changed times. In the early days he affected a brown velvet jacket, the baggiest of trousers and a monstrously gnarled stick. It was in this garb that he adorned the editorial office of a weekly review in which his unsigned editorials on the nationalization of milk and kindred topics were hardly less admired than the poems and sketches which he contributed over his own name to the literary section. The latter were collected and appeared as his first book, in a small edition which he has so successfully suppressed that his American admirers cherish the few copies obtainable at a price exceeding his total monthly income at this period. His wife still has a file of the review containing those anonymous political writings which eventually secured him an important post on a London paper. It was then that he acquired the leisure in which to write the books upon which his claim to fame—and eventually to American royalties—was to rest. At the same time, by one of those benign dispensations of Providence, owing to his position as literary editor and the innumerable ramifications which he gradually established in the English, he also acquired a network of influence which materially assisted his career as an established author. It became impossible for an unfavorable review of any book of his to appear, because almost every possible reviewer was under obligations to

him, or entertained hopes of him in his editorial
capacity. The clipping from the London press
which accompanied the offer of his works in
America naturally impressed the colonial mind and
in due course he achieved the dignity of a New
York imprint.

Even then, however, it cannot be said that his
American public more than vaguely existed in the
background of his consciousness. For one thing, he
was too busy consolidating his home defenses to
trouble about so distant a front. For another, he
really had no public in this country, as his too
confiding publisher discovered when the books about
which so many nice words were said in London were
jobbed off to the second-hand dealers in New York.
Subconsciously he reacted to the discouraging half-
yearly statement of his American sales by reënforc-
ing his conviction that this was a barbarous country
which produced no literature of its own and could
not be expected to appreciate a genuine work of
literature when confronted with it. His reviewing
staff had a free hand where American authors were
concerned, and the patronizing or abusive articles
that resulted were some compensation for injuries
received. Not that this matter very seriously concerned him, for by now his position in London was
assured, and Prime ministers' week-ends knew him
as a welcome guest. He moved in the smartest
society where literature was never sordid "shop"
but always the natural adjustment of the well-
educated English gentleman—or lady, for here he
was privileged to assist at the first flutterings of
authorship in young women whose social graces
covered a multitude of literary sins. This was

vastly more amusing than his relations with a few survivors, now repentant feminists, from the remote period when these ladies had begun. to live their own lives by sharing in the great adventure of his beginnings as a man of letters.

As he said himself, it was rather a bore when the war came and disturbed this pleasant existence. Fortunately, his social success was such that it never became necessary for him to contemplate actual service. Like all his friends, he had to adjust his vocabulary to the changed situation, and he did this so effectively that he soon found himself attached to a propaganda department. Innocent as he was of any language but his own, he seemed peculiarly fitted to undertake journalistic missions to the heathen of neutral Europe who could never, unaided, have realized the true significance of the great struggle. Thus he passed those hectic years armed with a weapon more lethal than a diplomatic passport, but with this he carried many a difficult position and fought the good fight to such purpose that decorations descended upon him almost as if he were an important profiteer. He guided the pens of foreign editorial writers, he organized bureaux of information and acquired such an intimate knowledge of European sleeping-cars and first-class continental hotels that his novels, to this day, are a proof that travel broadens the mind. His brochures and pamphlets were masterpieces of the kind, and it was generally felt in official circles that his combination of literary skill and good form was worth the bones of a hundred temporary gentlemen in uniform. He was especially skillful in his treatment of the problem of American intervention, possessing just that mixture of contempt and condescension which is the heritage of the true Briton in his relations with the Colonies. At the same time, he knew how to appeal to a sentimentality which he perfectly understood but did not share. When America finally answered the call of the mother country his feelings were comparable to those of the country squire when the tenants have voted as His Lordship wished—dignified rather than exuberant approval.

It was a fitting reward that he should experience in his own person a revelation analagous to that which he had labored so patriotically to effect. He, too, became aware of the existence of these States as a source of help in time of trouble. When the lull of the Permanent Peace came he was no longer the insular Englishman. He had traveled and lectured and preached to the barbarians, and it occurred to him that he might turn his war-developed talents to his own account. His London publisher concurred in the view that his American public would like to see him, and with admirable resolution he decided to go over and see what those weird Americans were like in their natural habitat. In Europe they had affected him as unpleasantly as the Anzacs, but the time had come to face the hardships imposed by his sense of duty to himself and to the fame of English letters. After certain delicate tests had been made by his New York and London publishers, new paragraphs began to percolate in propitious places announcing that this distinguished man of letters was about to visit America on a lecture tour.

His British reserve was a little strained by the

first terrific impact of the New World upon his consciousness. The reporters who met him on the
steamer extracted from him the inevitable words of
admiration, tempered with advice, which he had
been prepared to utter. He declared modestly that
he had read nothing of American literature since
Poe, but he added that America could not expect
to make any real contribution to the arts so long
as her attention was concentrated on the sordid
business of making money. The pursuit of the
dollar, he felt, should be left to other and older
races peculiarly fitted by ties of kinship and centuries of cultured tradition for the task. He added
a few words concerning the dire need of American
idealism to help in the rebuilding of Europe, and
hinted that, with the coöperation of the two great
branches of the Anglo-Saxon family, the League of
Nations should achieve those ideals for which England and America had fought in the Great War.

He languished only a night or two in a New
York hotel, for he soon discovered that a host of
cultured women had planned to provide him with
the lavish Transatlantic equivalents of those house-
parties which he enjoyed so much at home. As he
never failed to remark: he was overwhelmed by
American hospitality. Cars, wives and daughters
were placed at his disposal, and within a week he
was calling several prominent Long Island hostesses
by their Christian names and had seen more copies
of his works on drawing-room tables than he could
ever hope to see at home, where his books flourished
chiefly amongst the nondescript fiction which the
circulating libraries purchase with an altogether
admirable catholicity of taste. He secretly con-

ceived an immense respect for these charming people who actually bought his books instead of prom-
ising to ask for them at the library.   When eager
young things pressed him to write an appropriate
sentiment in a treasured volume he autographed it
with a gracious seriousness which persuaded all but
the most skeptical that he had done this sort of
thing before for privileged people and knew the
value of his signature.   In a letter to his London
publisher he made arrangements to have a limited,
large-paper edition of his forthcoming book signed
by the author.   "The Americans will take it off
your hands," he said reassuringly.

His public appearances were a huge success and
his agent soon had mapped out a tour which covered the whole country and brought him in a sum
in excess of anything he had dared to hope.   He
looked so distinguished that the women just adored
him; he was so unlike the crude type of their own
men who never really looked like creative artists.
His subjects, too, were so illuminating.   At the
P. E. N. Club he addressed an appeal to all concerned for closer relations between America and
England and dwelt upon the bond of language as
the greatest factor in establishing an Anglo-Saxon
peace.   His lecture on "Is there an American literature?", which he repeated in every place he visited,
was particularly stimulating.   After an appreciative
reference to Emerson and Longfellow he would discuss with real feeling the danger to American literature of straying from the straight path of Anglo-
Saxon tradition, and, without mentioning individuals, he would deprecate the rise of a school of
writers whose very names betrayed their alien out-

look. By audiences composed of the loveliest
daughters of Zion, for the most part, this Nordic
æsthetic was as warmly welcomed as by the professors of literature who presided, and who wrote
appreciative studies of the man and his work in the
Sunday supplements.

He could be relied upon for any occasion, from
a Wanamaker Book Week to a Book and Play
Luncheon, from an address to the Sulgrave Manor
Society to a reading at the Thanatopsis Club of
Davenport, Iowa; he could even carry off a debate
with a rival from England at the National Arts
Club without mishap, but he never talked without
a fee in accordance with the terms of his contract.
For a time he found it possible to evade specific
questions which would reveal his complete indifference towards current American literature and his
unalterable conviction that, with the possible excep-
tion of O. Henry, this country had nothing to offer.
In due course, however, he came into contact with
some of his American contemporaries, and with
truly British acumen set himself to exploit them for
his own ends. The art of publicity, as understood in
this country, being now familiar to him, he realized
the importance of cultivating American authors who
would advertise him by word of mouth or in print.
Thus he would allow himself occasionally to become interested in a work whose sales could never
be large in England, or whose success could in no
wise clash with that of his own work. For such he
would write a preface, or more frequently, a com-
mendatory paragraph in a London paper. With
the writer personally he would, in a few hours,
achieve a degree of affectionate intimacy utterly at

variance with his practice at home. I have known him to write letters to a casual American acquaintance in such terms of friendliness as he would be ashamed to betray to his oldest friend from college days in England. His reserves as a strong, silent Englishman vanish under the stress and urge of this very personal Anglo-American friendship, which is the goal he has substituted for the wider and more disinterested service of war time.

In this fashion the new type of literary visitor has evolved from his—in every sense—rude forbears whose harsh strictures on American life belong to the classical literature of Anglo-American relations. The voice has changed, but the hand is still the same that held the pen of Mrs. Trollope and Mr. Dickens. The pilgrim, modern style, keeps to himself the thoughts which his predecessors ingenuously committed to print. He hitches his wagon to the League of Nations, or to Sulgrave Manor, and proceeds to feed the national appetite for ideals while his own energies are concentrated on more realistic aims. He reserves for the private ear of his own people his impressions of colonial manners and customs and instead of becoming facetious about cuspidors and ice water, he will now write an essay entitled "American Poetry of To-Day," which proves on examination to be merely a sniffish review of a book of verse by some minor New England poet. This revised form of the old condescension is irresistible evidence of the dawn of a brighter day in the literary relations of the two countries. The incorrigible persistence of the American language is still a delicate subject and even the most tactful English commentators cannot refrain from pointing out that it is "incorrect" to say trolley when one means tram. When faced with an American translation of colloquial speech the conviction still surges up in the British mind that it is blasphemous to write: "Say, kid, how do you get that way?" when the slang of the original text demands it, but that the laws of God are obeyed when it is rendered: "I say, you priceless old bean, aren't you rather going off the deep end?"

Out of the sorrow and suffering of the Great War, however, the Island Race has emerged with a wider and deeper sense of the infinite possibilities of this great Republic. The literary pilgrim has a mission to do for himself what his country did in her hour of need. He has mastered the technique, and if here and there his natural inhibitions and prejudices peep out, his willingness for closer co-operation and mutual service is wholly admirable. With what graciousness he submits to the frank democratic friendliness of his American hero-worshipers, he who shuns the common herd at home, and is rather proud of the fact that most of his colleagues are personally unknown to him. In New York, it is now possible for one English author to meet another in a spirit of the purest human camaraderie, so perfectly do they adapt themselves to the freer atmosphere of the New World. The lesson of Armageddon—as they used to call it in the old propaganda days—has not been lost upon them; they realize that sweet are the uses of publicity. Pinning their faith in a few platitudes to carry them through the intellectual wilds of America, the literary pilgrims set out for the land that promises royalties and lecture fees. And each time they turn eastward, with their income tax returns skillfully adjusted and duly stamped at the Custom House, their hearts are filled with gratitude. They depart with tangible evidence that the pursuit of the dollar in America is not incompatible with the liveliest interest in the arts. It all depends upon who does the pursuing.

12. A WEST BRITON

THE West Briton is the near Englishman, the counterpart of the synthetic Gael. He is a more elusive phenomenon, and does not reveal himself so easily to the inexpert eye. As befits the torch-bearer in Ireland of English good form, he shrinks from exteriorization, and does not flaunt, as a rule, his acquired characteristics. At an early stage in his development he may betray some sartorial leanings in the direction of pseudo-Bond Street, but a glance at the genuine product is enough to discredit the Dublin substitute. It is not by such trifles that we have come to know the West Briton, for beneath the livery of Pope and Bradley—nay, even the sacred khaki itself—may beat a heart filled with an aggressive pride in Ireland. Not until the West Briton becomes articulate is it possible for the scientific investigator to determine the identity of the species. The voice is the first clew, for the West British accent is an exotic no less strange to English phonetics than to our own ears the pidgin Irish of the imported Gael. It is a slow and tortured procession of adenoidal sounds, the hybrid product of the miscegenation of English and Irish vowels. The youthful West Briton returns from his education abroad with this sort of vocal tattoo mark upon him, much as sailors bring back upon the arms and chest ocular demonstrations of the devilries of life in foreign parts.

Accent, however, is merely a primary symptom,

as the expert knows, since experiments in recent years have proved that there are authentic Irish Irelanders addicted to the pronunciation of an imaginary "r" at the end of such words as Maria and idea. These returned natives have attained in exile to refinements which elude the vast majority of home-grown West Britons, who have all the difficulty in the world in suppressing that letter where it legitimately occurs. Consequently, it is to the substance, rather than to the form, that we must look for irrefutable evidence of West Britonism. No profound psycho-analysis is needed to discover that complex. The simplest key-words will suffice to produce the reactions which tell so much to the scientific observer. For example:

Word	*Response*
Sinn Féin	Pro-German
Irish	Vulgar
England	Mother-country
Green	Red
Nationality	Disloyalty
Patriotism	O.B.E.
Self-determination	Czecho-Slovakia

The West Briton has none of the introspective doubts which occasionally disturb the Britisher of intelligence. His motto is: "England, right or wrong." In the place where his soul ought to be, something shudders at the mere thought of nationalism. It is not cultivated in Ireland, he thinks, by the right sort of people. It is incurably vulgar and low class, and is obviously designed for the servants. The only point on which he would agree with Sir Horace Plunkett is that Irishmen should forget Anglo-Irish history. The pseudo-Englishman has saved himself that effort by never learning it. He suspects everything Irish unless it has been approved of by his English friends, and where the interests of the two countries clash, he echoes his favorite newspaper in declaring it unthinkable to "every decent Irishman" that Ireland should come first. Every national effort, of whatever kind, is either ignored or despised by the West Briton, until he finds that English opinion is interested, then, if he can, he will take charge of the matter and devitalize it to extinction.

In West British circles there is a dread of "politics" which the uninitiated have some difficulty in understanding. That so essentially a political creation as the West Briton should frown on politics suggests a paradox, but it is merely a question of definitions. To him all things Irish are tainted with politics. Thus when he, in the exuberance of his loyalty, wraps himself in the Union Jack and chaunts "Rule Britannia" on some occasion of rejoicing to England—that is simply a non-partisan demonstration of imperial patriotism. Should the majority of his fellow-countrymen elect to indulge in any corresponding exhibition of Irish patriotic feeling, he is pained by the introduction of "politics," and is uneasy until a few tanks dispose of the disaffected agitators. As West Britain sees it, political freedom and freedom from politics are alike ensured by the free expression of strictly minority opinions. That is the condition so felicitously described as the enjoyment of the same privileges as the other parts of the Empire. A most expensive dispensation of Providence (by special arrangement with Dublin Castle) has enabled this Barmecide feast of liberty to be spread in Ireland to the honor and profit of the West Briton. His Press, his bureaucracy, and his divines flourish with an impunity so amazing that, when the worms turn, once in a century, he is easily stampeded by the horror of novelty into shrill appeals for assistance in crushing them.

That there is always so ready a response to this call is a tribute to the West Briton's conception of his own importance. Yet, there cannot be many educated Englishmen who derive any satisfaction from the existence of this hyphenated citizen, who is a voluntary alien in his own country and a ridiculous provincial in England. It is not as if he were a satisfactory substitute for his model. His sole achievement is to render England absurd at best, and hateful at worst, to those who have no opportunity of comparing the real with the imitation. The West Briton cultivates all that is cheapest in England, and aggravates the offense by the addition of the worst features of his own unculture. It is a salutary experience for a cultivated Englishman to plumb the depths of West British barbarism. There he finds a spectacle of fatuous provincialism, of complacent reaction, from which he turns away to hide either his laughter or his disgust. The West Briton is an unfriendly caricature, the *reductio ad absurdum* of the least attractive English characteristics. When he leaves Ireland he seems to become vaguely aware of this, and he finds it advisable to dissemble by playing the part of an elephantine Irishman. He is then conscious of his lack of national identity; he feels that he is a species of *parvenu*, and to conceal his discomfiture he does a little Irish clowning.

The best that can be said for the West Briton is that the species is becoming slowly extinct. At great cost Ireland has gradually destroyed the nests in which these creatures breed, and the disappearance of each tribe has been greeted with no tears in either England or Ireland. In fact, once a clearance has been effected, Englishmen are apt to call upon us to be grateful for their reluctant coöperation, and to claim the result as a benefit voluntarily conferred. Deprived of artificial nourishment, the West Briton must either die or revert to the natural habits of the race from which he is sprung. He usually prefers the latter alternative, the more so as the last five years have accustomed him to strange adventures. For the first time in his history, nationalism became respectable, small nationalities were transformed into controlled products and ceased to be the monopoly of humanitarians and rebels. Nationalists no longer lingered in the offices of obscure societies, or in the drawing rooms of emancipators who collected oppressed natives. They became as valuable to politicians as a terminological inexactitude, and were as familiar to the bureaucracy as a parliamentary Commission. West Britain knew of really nice people who mixed with nationalists, even Irish nationalists, but that, of course, was a temporary excess of enthusiasm, and had to be mitigated. Nevertheless, a process of familiarization was initiated which has not been without its effect upon the younger generation of West Britons. These have been guilty of heresies which, granted favorable conditions, should be productive, and the auspices are favorable. Soon a wax effigy of a typical West Briton will be placed at Madame Tussaud's, and a gramophone record of his voice, intoning the first leader of "The Irish Times," will be lodged in the Museum for the enlightenment of posterity by the Irish Free State.

13. A SYNTHETIC GAEL

HE is unmistakably a synthetic Gael. His kilt and his Oxford accent proclaim it. Not that the mere Irishman, speaking English as usual, is permitted to judge this accent in the mutual exchange of their common tongue, for he speaks only Irish. But above the disguise of slender consonants and the attempted *blas* there pierce the shrill or nasal tones of refined Cockney, painfully obvious to all ears but those of the resolutely patriotic. The latter feel, to some extent, responsible for this extravagant figure and conspire to protect him from realistic criticism. All the chivalry of the Irish race wells up at so grand a spectacle, the Irish-speaking Cockney, whose ruthless volubility bestrews the Grand Old Tongue with the wreckage of mangled consonants and distorted vowels. There is in this attitude a suspicion of that suppressed respect of the subject nation for one of their conquerors, for the Doers, the Yea-sayers, who rush, not in, but out, where the little angels of nationality would not dare to tread. In this onslaught upon the speech of the Gael one perceives something of the spirit which has made England what she is. The imported Gael is truly a boy of the bulldog breed. His not to reason why, his but to speak, or die, when he finds this new world to conquer.

The synthetic Gael lends a note of color pleasantly exotic in this city of the Pale, this English-speaking Dublin, which is nevertheless more Irish than our East Britons. Enter the club or drawing-room where the intelligentsia are gathered together, in the name of Kathleen ni Houlihan. The flow of conversation is apparently endless, for there is always much to be set down in malice while one or other of the company keeps an ear attentive for the possible approach of the subject of all this innocent merriment. If there is none absent of those whose lives are the subjects of these ingenuous scandals, then there always remains the grander theme of Ireland. There will be some present whose part in the secular crusade for freedom has already been inscribed by auto-penmanship upon the historic scroll. Others, whose share in that great adventure is even more important, are discreetly screened from public knowledge of their claims to fame. They may provide the good listeners for those elo-quent prophets of a New Order, those restless analysts of the existing dispensation, whatever it may be, whose nightly *ante mortem* examinations of the case are the best proof of the patient's inten-tion of recovering.

Suddenly into this babel of talk there stalks the near-Gael, the synthetic Irishman, and a hush falls upon the innocent natives, conscious of their mod-ern nether garments and *Weltsprache*. *Conus tá do shláinte?* he may inquire, as he shakes hands, *à l'anglaise*, with an embarrassed host, whom he envelops in a cloud of words from the curious dia-lect Cockney-Irish. As often as not the unhappy Irishman makes some attempt to divert our friend's attention into the broad stream of English, but enthusiasm knows no law, not even that of politeness, and the reply comes in the *Ersatz* tongue, which retains only the incongruous intonations of the speaker's native Oxford, or thereabouts. Perhaps, as a concession to a weaker brother, speech is supplemented by pantomime, in the hope of staving off the now inevitable triumph of an alien culture. At this point the host will retire discomfited to gather up the threads of interrupted discussion, and this is taken as a signal that the English offensive may be resumed. Whispered conversations now emerge defiantly, and the Gael is abandoned to his own resources. He has happily discovered some defenseless patriot, whose vague dalliance with O'Growney's Grammar, together with a certain lack of moral courage, exposes him to an all-too-friendly enemy. Going over the top with a cry which sounds like *Lá breagh*, he is soon lost in the philological No Man's Land, cowering beneath a hail of Direct Method phrases. Perhaps in the end he can take cover behind a *go raibh maith agat*, as he disappears in the mephitic clouds of smoke, which proclaim the presence of an Irish cigar. At all events, it is safe to paraphrase Dante and add: that day he talked no more. It is not until the Gael has cried *Slán leat*, and has been comforted on his departure with a few half-boastful *Slán agat*, in response, that the company can wholeheartedly resume the congenial business of demonstrating how admirably the English language can be turned to the advantage of Irish nationality.

It is not, however, in the cities of the Pale that the synthetic Gael can hope to do more than register his protest, and incidentally exhibit those qualities of dogged courage and tenacity, that faculty of

never knowing when he is beaten, which, like the
Battle of Waterloo, he has won on the playing fields
of Eton. It is his custom to venture at intervals
into the districts which are wholly or partly inhab-
ited by native Irish speakers. There the immodesty
of his costume is liable to create a sensation which
is a confirmation of his reiterated belief in the
purity of the Irish race. Unfortunately, it seems
to be impossible to kill two birds with one kilt, for
the vindication of his views as to the purity of the
race is obtained at the expense of his success as the
returned native. His naked knees do not inspire
confidence in his linguistic mission. Moreover, he
is already too seriously handicapped by his improvi-
sations of idiom and pronunciation. He is fated
to hear the language which he thought he was
leaving behind him when he crossed the Irish Sea,
changing his speech—to some extent—but not his
soul. Here then is the challenge which he cannot
refuse. The atavistic call of the blood arouses him;
he thinks imperially and acts accordingly. He con-
ceives, that is to say, a moral, religious duty; a
patriotic trust is imposed upon him; he owes a responsibility to civilization. He will insist upon the
obedience of the mere native, who simply must be
bullied into speaking Irish. Even if these back-
ward creatures cannot understand the Gaelic equivalent of the French of Stratford-at-Bow, they will
be no worse off than the recipients of imperial culture elsewhere, who hear a great number of remarkable utterances, whose purport is invariably obscure
in its immediate application. In fact, comprehension is, on the whole, undesirable, for it frequently
involves complications.

The Gael's life, in the main, is a happy one, for there always comes the day when he can live dangerously. He can refuse to speak English to some indubitably Irish policeman or, in some analogous way, exercise the right of every true-born Briton to make himself as objectionable as possible to the representatives of the State. Being a citizen of the Gaelic State, he may not see the situation in this light, he may not recognize that the voice is the voice of Herbert Spencer, although the hand is the hand of his brother. He proceeds, therefore, to subject the coldest of cold monsters to the same treatment as his amiable friends and acquaintances have learned to accept. Alas, the State, although it provides for the teaching of Irish, does not feel the same moral responsibility for the synthetic Gael, the by-product of that teaching, as his adopted countrymen do. They, as we know, are not insensible to the flattery of this tangible proof of their success in propaganda. Even the risk of Cockneyfied Irish does not frighten them, for did not the Normans impose themselves markedly upon England, but the linguistic traces of their passage have not interfered with the final triumph of English over French? The State, in consequence, is apt to treat our synthetic patriot as the Americans treat their hyphenated citizens. They make the Gael, who would normally be merely absurd, irresistible. It endows him with all those divine rights which are the prerogative in Ireland of every victim of official stupidity. The crime of *lèse patrie* may be invoked to silence his critics.

Few Irishmen would be so ungrateful as to criticize the Gael. Has he not the courage of his con-

victions? So long as England supplies these living
proofs of the separate national existence of Ireland,
the Irish separatist can concern himself with his real
business. The pomps and fripperies of nationality,
the kilts and shawls, may be left to the sentimen-
talists who like that sort of thing, while English
costumes and the English language suffice for men
engaged upon sterner tasks. Both have been employed with that sublime disregard for trifles which
is characteristic of great men. Can one imagine
John Mitchel wasting the opportunities which his
command of English gave him in order to engage
in Ollendorfian interchanges with some coy Aran
Islander, or some recalcitrant poet of the Anglo-
Irish renascence? The idea is as absurd as that of
an Emmet or a Wolfe Tone throwing away upon
the village constable the chance of incarceration
provided by a refusal to give his name in English.
No, the professional Gael's part is that of a re-
tainer, or of a human trophy attached to the
chariot of Irish nationalism. Villiers de l'Isle
Adam said: "As for living, our servants will do
that for us." In the same spirit Irishmen must feel
that it is meet that we should import foreigners to
do the things we have no time to do. The Gael is
there to show what we could be if we tried. He
brings to his self-imposed mission a solemnity of
which we like to think ourselves incapable. The
stuff of which empires are made is in his bones. I
can imagine him adapting the lines of Rupert
Brooke:

> If I should die, think only this of me:
> That there's some corner of a foreign tongue
> That is for ever Englished. . . .

But Ireland will see to it that this dream shall be
defeated.   Meanwhile it is by no means a small
feat to have harnessed that impulse to the purposes
of the Irish nation.   The synthetic Gael is a slight
revenge for the West Briton.

Interlude

14. ENTER THE AUTHOR

WHEN the first chapter in this series of Imaginary Portraits appeared in "The American Mercury," it became the occasion of a display of literary manners so peculiarly in harmony with the Ku Kluxing, Fascista world in which we have been living since the Great Peace befell us, that I have obtained Mr. Burton Rascoe's permission to reprint, by way of an epilogue, his account of the incident, as published in the New York "Tribune" at the time.

I ought, however, to explain that the facts upon which Mr. Rascoe so gracefully embroiders are all true. I was called to the telephone one evening by a gentleman completely unknown to me, who gave his name as Malcolm Cowley, and who requested me peremptorily to allow him to see me. His business, he declared, was to talk over certain aspects of my "Æsthete: Model 1924." I told him that I had no desire to discuss my public statements in private with a person whom I did not know, and that it was quite inconceivable to me that anything I had written could merit the supplementary effort of a debate of this kind. Whereupon Mr. Cowley expressed his opinion of me in language so filthy that, when his oaths and obscenities were exhausted, I asked him if he had not written a poem for one of the esoteric magazines with the modern æsthetes' weakness for what is dirty. Upon which, Mr. Cowley offered to come around and "beat me up." For a week or more Mr. Malcolm Cowley, Mr. Matthew Josephson, Mr. Kenneth Burke and others, male and female, telephoned me at frequent intervals, repeating the threats and abuse which had first indicated to me that something was rotten in the state of Greenwich Village. Anonymous telegrams, facetious and abusive, also arrived, but, owing to the pruderies of the Western Union Telegraph Company, these could not be expressed in the same vigorous, hooligan style as the telephone messages. In these I had begun to take an interest entirely apart from the amusement which they at first afforded me. I discovered the names of more outraged æsthetes than even I, in my pessimism, had suspected, and I received the most dramatic confirmation of my generalizations concerning the type, for the most abusive, the most positive that their personal lives and intimate secrets had been betrayed by me, were precisely those of whom I knew nothing, until their oaths were so obligingly transmitted by the New York Telephone Company. Another burden was added to my life, however, for I have since made it my business to read the writings of these inglorious, but never, I regret to say, mute Miltons, the lewd forefathers of the literature and art that are to obliterate from human memory the rude and clumsy efforts of the past.

I should hate to leave this matter under a cloud of obscenities and threats. Gentle hearts, it seems, do beat beneath the rugged breasts of these literary coalheavers. Thus, the toughest and most militant —from a distance—finally sent me the following graceful apology:

"Please excuse me for having used such extravagant language to describe you. I only meant to say that you were a sneak, a coward and a liar.
In this description of your character, fortunately, the two of us seem to agree.
"Sincerely yours,
"MALCOLM COWLEY."

Pressing this bouquet to my bosom, I step back into the wings, and make way for Burton Rascoe:

"Toward the end of the year 1923, during the reign of Calvin the Cool, a hard-working linguist and critic, named, we shall say (for purposes of concealment), Ernest Boyd, racked his brains through the forepart of a long night for an idea which he might blow into a sizeable article he had promised the editors for the first number of 'The American Mercury.' This Boyd was a mild gentleman, habitually clad in somber brown from shoes to hat, who (so far as appearance goes) would have done rather better than Anton Lang in the chief rôle of the Oberammergau Passion Play. He was given to indignations, but only of a scholarly character: an error in translation would fever him with a terrible animus, and a misquotation, however harmless, would make his blood boil. Toward other matters, social, moral or political, he maintained a complete indifference: so long as men did not attribute to Basius Secundus sentiments which had actually been uttered by Aristides, of Smyrna, and did not misconstrue in translation the exact meaning of a phrase, it mattered not a whit to him how they cast their votes, what beliefs they subscribed to or what breaches of decorum they were in the habit of observing.

"He was a man of vast learning, who spoke with ease and fluency no less than thirty languages and dialects, both ancient and modern, including Gaelic and American. His interest in literature and erudition was singularly pure: it contained no adulterate of moral fervor or political parti-pris; it was a voracious and consuming passion: he read with impartial eagerness everything that got into print—complete issues, every word, of the 'Dial,' 'Broom,' 'Bookman,' 'Yale Review,' 'Vanity Fair,' 'S4N,' 'TNT,' 'The Pagan,' 'La Nouvelle Revue Française,' 'The Westminster Gazette,' 'Variety,' 'Zit's,' 'Mercure de France,' 'Revue des Deux Mondes,' 'The Irish Statesman,' 'The New Republic,' 'The Freeman,' 'The Nation,' 'The Double-Dealer,' 'The Wave,' 'The Reviewer,' 'Die Zukunft,' the complete issues, want ads and all of the Sunday papers, every book review and literary article published on the European Continent and in the dominions of Great Britain, including 'The Peking & Tientsin Times.'

"The postal authorities found it necessary to assign a special dray and employ three piano movers to make the daily deliveries of bales of reading matter at Boyd's address on the fifth floor of an apartment building in East Nineteenth Street. Authors, eager for an American audience through translation, sent him their new books as fast as they came off the presses in Paris, Berlin, Budapest, Milan, Seville, Athens, Bucharest, Copenhagen, Stockholm, Nijni-

Novgorod, Tronjhem, Warsaw, Bremen, Calcutta, Vienna, The Hague, Amsterdam, Geneva, Marseilles and Cologne. Four thicknesses of books lined the walls from floor to ceiling in every room, closet and hallway. Books, paper bound and in boards, cloth and parchment, were piled under the beds, tables and bath tubs; they were hung from the ceiling in hammocks; piles of them served as a dining table and still other piles of them served as chairs; the building in which this vast accumulation of reading matter was lodged sank three feet out of plumb under the strain, and steel supports had to be leveled against the walls to keep a flood of books from inundating the environs of Gramercy Park.

"To the business of reading this avalanche of printed words, Boyd addressed himself with meticulous conscientiousness. Nothing escaped him; if some poor hack of a scribbler in the back pages of 'Le Monde Nouveau' wrote a paragraph about Jack London under the impression that London was still alive, or some hurried piecework translator innocently followed a misprint in a Latin-American novel, Boyd would know about it and would take it as in the nature of a personal outrage.

"He was a great purist in diction, and he cherished the quaint notion that prose and poetry should make sense. This notion put him to great inconvenience and plagued his nights with wrathful distempers; for he was bound to keep up his reading, and a great deal of the stuff in the more advanced reviews—both prose and poetry—didn't make sense. Part of its charm lay in its naïve or intentional mystification. It was the interesting vogue of the day for writers, critics as well as poets, to put down words or sounds, even if the sounds did not fit any word in the vocabulary, just as they came out of their heads, without order or sequence. Thus, some of the most cried-up poetry of the day, both in France and in America, was poetry in which words were dispensed with altogether and geometrical designs were worked out with such typographical devices as c @ / ? ! % ‡ " & $ (- ; and). Thus, a musical critic, a very cultured man of exquisite sensibility, discarded the idea that criticism is comment and sought to convey to his readers, through the media of words the exact sensations visited upon his sensitivity by the sounds Mr. Ornstein evoked from the piano. This was a worthy enterprise, and the critic was successful in it in the case of quite a handful of readers. It can hardly be counted to this music critic's discredit if Boyd and a great number of others did not possess a sensitive apparatus identical with that of the music critic and were uncomprehending and discourteous enough to refer to such musical criticism as nonsense. Then, too, there were some earnest and eager young men who began to feel that the English language was in a bad way and needed to be shaken up a bit. Their preoccupation was with rhythm and cadence—at least they used these words very frequently—and with form, rather than with matter. They achieved some rather astonishing feats with words in this shaking up; but in the end their preoccupation did not stand them in good stead, for when they came to explain their aims to the multitude in the sequential order of words which the multitude could understand, their words had a habit of reading along all right, but without conveying any meaning. These young men seemed to have lost the faculty of making sense altogether. This was especially unfortunate, because they began to fight among themselves about their theories only to find that they were equally as unintelligible to one another as they had been to the general public. The result was a lamentable confusion, with denials, recriminations, prayers to St. Guillaume Apollinaire, references to Lessing, invocations of Tristran Tzara, and echoes of arguments from the nuts of the Café de la Rotonde.

"Boyd, ever a glutton for printed words, tried to follow all this. The stuff seethed in his brain, giving him nightmares and nervous disorders. Misprints and faulty quotations, sewer French, badly mangled and incoherent English, expressionism without expression and Modernists fighting among themselves about the writings and aims of foreign writers they imperfectly comprehended—all this gave Boyd the jim-jams. Then a strange thing happened. Flagellating his cerebral cortices for the article he had promised the editors of 'The American Mercury,' his phantasmagoria of impressions began to synthesize and assume shape in a composite picture which he sketched out and entitled 'Æsthete: Model 1924.'

"Two hours after the edition of the magazine appeared on the stands Greenwich Village was in an uproar. The whole literary left wing, which had hitherto been disorganized by internecine strife, solidified against the perpetrator of the article. Obscure poets and art theorists who had never been heard of before began collaring people and calling them up on the phone, saying that Boyd had themselves especially in mind when he wrote the piece and that they meant to have his blood. The progress of literature was deemed to have been stopped by the article and American culture set back a hundred years. The whole edition was gobbled up within ten hours and another edition put on the presses: most of the readers were young writers who assumed at once that they had been personally and specifically libeled in the article. East Nineteenth Street swarmed with the younger poets, and when the venerable Boyd set out on his morning constitutional he was greeted with a fusillade of ripe tomatoes, riper eggs, sticks, stones and copies of 'S4N,' and barely escaped back into his house with his life. There he was kept a prisoner by expediency for three days while Dadaists pushed his door bell, kept his telephone abuzz, scaled the walls to his apartment and cast old cabbages and odor bombs through the windows, sent him denunciatory telegrams, and rigged up a radio receiving outfit with an amplifier through which they broadcast the information that he was a liar, sneak, thief, coward and no gentleman. When one of the poets let loose to Boyd over the telephone a string of vilely obscene abuse Boyd mistook the recital for one of the poet's poems, and so only further infuriated the poet without giving him satisfaction, whereupon the poet challenged Boyd to a fist fight, and when Boyd declined the invitation the poet spent $64 for telegrams to important personages who knew nothing about the article and nothing about the signer of the telegram and very little, if anything, about Boyd, declaring that Boyd was a disgrace to humanity. Barricaded behind his books, subsisting on depleted rations and grown wan and weary under the assaults and harass-

ments, Boyd called Heaven to witness that he had
never heard of or read anything by any one of some
dozens of his most revengeful assailants and that
they had read into his article hints about their private life which he had no intention of putting there
nor on re-reading could discover. . . ."

REAL

Impressions

15. H. L. MENCKEN

WHEN I first saw him he immediately satisfied my European desire for the Transatlantic exotic, as he sat beside a typewriter in a tiny room, filled with the reports of vice commissions and a strange host of Baptist, Methodist, Presbyterian, Prohibition and New Thought journals; his file of "The Congressional Record" as well thumbed as a priest's breviary. In a corner stood a 100% American cuspidor, a reassuring piece of local color to my ingenuous eyes.

In that round, good-humored face, lit up with mischievous joy at the daily spectacle of triumphant democracy, in those bluest of roguish eyes, I could see nothing of the Nietzschean monster who is the H. L. Mencken of popular legend. To me he seemed a bulky, Rabelaisian figure, full of laughter and kindly malice, enormously energetic, and ceaselessly in pursuit of intellectual sport. After the somewhat hirsute and class-conscious intellectuals I had only recently left behind me in Europe, this man in his conventional business suit and starched collar impressed me. As he talked, he constantly stroked back a wisp of hair which refused to lie correctly, and this gesture was an incongruous reminder of the grander sweep of the younger Yeats tossing back a rebellious lock from his forehead, a

lock of which only the rudiments remain since the
Irish poet was tonsored by the Dalilah of convention.

"My aim is to combat by ridicule and invective
American piety and stupidity and tin-pot morality: progressives, professional moralists, patriots,
Methodists, osteopaths, Christian Scientists, social-
ists, single-taxers and advocates of the initiative,
the referendum and the recall. In brief, the whole
doctrine of democracy." In the course of his remarks my ears were tickled by a whole armory of
epithets—boozehounds, boy snouts, literary pall-
bearers, virtuosi of virtue, chemical purity, malig-
nant morality—which are part of the delight in the
rush of words and their invention which marks his
affinity to Rabelais. "I have advocated a tax of a
dollar a day on bachelors, on the ground that it is
worth it to be free, and I have drafted laws providing for the assassination of public officials and
the regulation and licensing of uplifters. I am in
favor of votes for women because it is the *reductio
ad absurdum* of democracy." He confessed he had
been beaten in all his campaigns, that he had written up to that time—1913—some 2,000,000 words
in the Baltimore "Evening Sun," and had been at-
tacked by at least 10,000 letters to the editor.

As he recounted the adventures of his soul among
democrats he had worn a rather charming expression of a naughty boy, but when I mentioned literature he looked serious, almost despondent. There
was Whitman, of course, and Poe, to whose hideous
and neglected tomb, a few blocks away from where
we sat, he directed me. Mark Twain, too, was not
the mere buffoon he was reputed to be. "You

know Frank Norris's 'McTeague'? A great book."
Dreiser was still viewed with alarm by the college
professors, but England had long since recognized
the merits of "Sister Carrie." "Dreiser is a genius,
but he doesn't know how to write, or when to stop."
Chicago, I would see, was the real literary capital
of the United States, the best work was coming
from the Middle West; Sherwood Anderson, Vachel
Lindsay and a number of other names, now as prominent as they were then obscure, were cited. But he
held out little hope, so long as the blight of Puritanism and democracy persisted. Once more his face
lit up combatively and he evoked his adversaries:
the snouters, the vice-crusaders, the prohibitionists,
the Comstocks, the right-thinkers, forward lookers
and viewers-with-alarm.

From a shelf of vice commission reports he took
one and showed it to me. These documents are all
valuable pieces of contemporary pornography and
bring high prices in the market, he assured me.
"This one was barred from the mails by a rival
pack of smuthounds. Dog eating dog!" With a
shout of contemptuous laughter he turned to his
desk. His great virtues of punctuality and conscientiousness in work asserted themselves. He was
going to jump into the arena again. As I closed
the door the rattle of his typewriter could be heard.
He had gone into action.

16. THEODORE DREISER

H E came forward to greet me out of the shadows of a long room, lit only by a couple of candles and the flickering flames from an open fireplace, in a typical Greenwich Village apartment, in the days before the war had exalted that quarter (and its rents!) far beyond the reach of the intellectual proletariat. A huge, ungainly figure, whose heavy features were relieved only by the alert and kindly glance of those observant eyes which have seen everything and forgotten nothing. The profile of Theodore Dreiser reminded me of the medallions of the later Roman emperors. This powerful, sensual face was thrown into relief by contrast with the pale, tender, almost Madonna-like young woman who came to tell us that dinner was served, and seated herself at the head of the table.

It was not until we had settled ourselves again in front of the fire that Theodore Dreiser began to talk. He had taken his handkerchief from his pocket, and this he rolled and unrolled and twisted unceasingly during the whole of the evening. The now familiar story of his early struggles with "Sister Carrie" was rehearsed, his editorship of a ladies' fashion paper, his strange apprenticeship to a novelette factory, where it was his business to find an old forgotten novel, tear it in half and write a new ending for the one fragment and a new beginning for the other. He denied that he had written under the influence of Zola, and asserted that "Sister Carrie" and "Jennie Gerhardt" were completed before he had read anything of the French Realists. He confessed a frank inability to explain the creative process in himself, and everything about him suggested a curious, naïve bewilderment at this flux of words and impressions, which insisted on pouring from him, but defied his control. He seemed as helpless when confronted with this gift of the fates as he was in the face of the persistent neglect and abuse which were at that time his portion at the hands of the vast majority of his countrymen. With gratitude he spoke of the encouragement he had received in England, and with bitter contempt he referred ever and again to his fight with the Puritans.

If it were not a paradox to describe the author of so many bulky volumes as inarticulate, I would say that my dominant impression of the man was his inarticulateness. When we turned from his own work to general topics he at once revealed that ingenuousness, that frantic groping for words, for self-expression, which expose his books to the gibes of little professors, but impress his admirers with a real sense of original force. Strenuously twisting his handkerchief, Dreiser would utter such apophthegms as: "Ah, what an inscrutable mystery is life!" Then, he would relapse into a slough of slatternly phrases, cliches, and commonplaces, from which one vaguely gathered that he had become aware that all was not right with the world, and that, perhaps, after all, God was not in His heaven. The class-conscious radicals were then just beginning to become aware of him as a scourge of Puritanism capable of being enrolled in the great fight for the Marxian millennium. I was unconsciously witnessing the transition of the ignored and neglected Dreiser from the authorship of authentic American fiction to that state of semi-martyrdom and conscious revolt which inevitably overtakes those whom the gods of Greenwich Village decide to exalt. This scrupulously impassive observer of life was about to become a commentator upon that sardonic and buffoonish spectacle at which he had gazed with puzzled but unflinching eyes to such good effect in "Sister Carrie," "Jennie Gerhardt" and "The Titan."

Nevertheless, it was dawn before I stood once more on the doorstep shaking hands with him, this interesting personality without a single personal idea. What had fascinated me was precisely that quality which gives his work its peculiar savor, the phenomenon of a wholly natural, native genius. The clay of this American soil still sticks to the feet of that son of the Middle West, who sees life as he saw Europe in "A Traveller at Forty," which reads as if a child had miraculously acquired the power to convey the wondering and chaotic impressions of its first contact with the adult world. Out of all those laborious platitudes on wealth and art and sex and economics, those proofs of technical helplessness in the art of writing, of selection, there emerged a picture of a man of unspoiled sensitiveness to the storm and stress of Nature, of an elemental energy and passionate desire to understand. Theodore Dreiser is a primitive, and his art must be measured in corresponding terms.

17. JAMES BRANCH CABELL

THIS gentleman from Virginia was in town, and we were to meet for dinner. First a search in the inappropriate depths of Greenwich Village for the subterranean restaurant chosen to entertain Mr. Cabell. A dreary place, below the street level, with sawdust on the floor, or at least, giving an impression of that rude carpeting. A long wait, during which two or three guests straggled in, an invocation to one of the party to assure the proprietor that we were "all right," and that he could dispense his usual hospitality. Disconsolate conclusions as to the reprehensible effects of Prohibition on the American palate, which showed no signs of revolt. . . . "Gentlemen, Mr. Cabell of Virginia."

A serious and clearly very shy man advances, smiles wanly and is soon absorbed in the problem of ordering from a menu long since conned and rejected by the earlier arrivals. The author of "Jurgen" is with us. A sober figure, in truth, with the formal manners of a country gentleman, but without the hearty, downright manner which might be expected from so *farouche* a devotee of open air and rural life. He wears glasses which give him the air of a lawyer; austere, old-fashioned glasses, which eschew the modernity, the intellectual connotations of tortoise-shell and its convincing substitutes. He says little. His demeanor is that of a layman, high in the favor of the reverend clergy, who is privileged to attend a meeting of the General Synod of the Episcopalian Church.

James Branch Cabell, Esquire, of Dumbarton Grange, Dumbarton, Virginia, a landed proprietor, doubtless; but no, this is the author of "Jurgen." Remember what Mr. Sumner thought of that rascally pawnbroker and his creator! How the flappers giggled over it! With what unanimous indignation we rallied to protest against interference with this emancipated artist, this champion of the freedom of letters, this victim of the fetich of respectability. A most respectable man, surely; quiet, dignified, embarrassed even by what little fame our having come there signified. Here is no Antichrist to stir the Puritan from his lethargy.

Mr. Cabell was an author before Mr. Sumner made him popular. He was, in fact, a most distinguished author, an ironist so fine that one could pity his fate in a country where irony is dreaded and misunderstood, resented as only children resent that intangible weapon which, unlike another and more familiar menace, hurts them more than it hurts us. There is nothing in the repose of those shy, handsome features to belie the satiric wit of "The Rivet in Grandfather's Neck"; in those gray eyes, behind their thoroughly English *pince-nez*, there is the mockery of "The Cream of the Jest." That strong forehead, dominating a stern thoughtful face, the streaks of gray in his hair, suggest the philosopher of "Beyond Life." What if he should have had the reputation of "Jurgen" thrust upon him? An unpardonable and heretical supposition, upon which

the whole race and breed of Cabellistas will pronounce anathema. . . .

We shall see. After dinner we journey up town
to a party—not too large, at Mr. Cabell's urgent
request—convened to do honor to the rare occasion
of one of these always deferred visits to New York.
We do not offer an equipage to the Southern gentleman; the Fifth Avenue stage is our democratic
coach, *la carrozza di tutti*, as Edmondo de Amicis
would say. Well, the champagne has been put on
ice, and we are moving in the right direction. Suddenly some commotion is perceptible, Mr. Cabell
is gazing anxiously about him. He must not stay
out late. He has a train to catch. He is expected
somewhere down on Long Island. He must leave
here. He is gone . . .

The party for Mr. Cabell continues; the reën-
forcements meet. The champagne is still on ice, but
the tinkle of a cocktail shaker beguiles the wait.
The attentive pupils of a professor dwell eagerly
on his words, strange, incongruous reminiscences of
class-room talks drift into the stifling air, as the
glorious classics are pulled from their shelves and
well-remembered passages are exhumed. It is long
past the latest hour when, it once seemed, we might
have enjoyed the company of Mr. Cabell. Late arrivals appear, one forgetful of all else but the never-
to-be-forgotten fact: James Branch Cabell is in
town. He is accompanied by the gayest young
thing imaginable. What is she to Cabell or Cabell
to her? . . . But, there is "Jurgen." Yes, she
knows it, you bet!

The moment is appropriate for the solemn festivity. Let us drink the champagne to our young visitor. It is evidently nothing in her young life. But she is polite. She drinks it. The champagne is flat. . . .

A few days later a charming note from Dumbarton Grange, in the exquisitely fine calligraphy of Mr. Cabell, who presents his apologies for his hasty departure. He thoroughly enjoyed what there was of the occasion. It really was the author of "Jurgen" who dined in town.

18. EUGENE O'NEILL

A WIRY figure, in a blue serge, double-breasted coat, with that indefinable air of restlessness, of being out of one's element, which is peculiar to seafaring men ashore. Eugene O'Neill no longer follows the sea, but it is not for nothing that the sea permeates all his best work. He is the wild, roving, adventurous, pessimistic, disillusioned, essentially unromantic spirit of the sailor, sublimated and rendered articulate. There is intense vitality in those sharp, black, shining eyes, that glitter as they dart from object to object. The smile is boyish in its charm; youth and vigor are here. Yet the hair is gray near his ears, and at first glance the face has an air that is curiously old, and haggard and worn; an optical illusion, but a significant one. This is not a literary gentleman, but a man whose struggles, passions and experiences just happen to make literature.

When he talks of himself, of life, he is arresting. His literary opinions are sound, independent and shrewd, so long as they do not touch on the contemporary experiments of the æstheticians in which he has become involved. Here his good sense and humor desert him. He becomes self-conscious, being no longer sure of his ground, but obviously impressed by the gift of words which does duty for ideas with some of his instructors in the art of not concealing art but of laboring it, which is the ultramodern style. He would be surprised and embar-

rassed—for modesty is the essence of the man—and
finally indignant, no doubt, if he were told that his
genius in the theater is being used by the æsthetic
vivisectionists, intent solely upon results of their
own, that his soaring imagination drags with it a
dead weight of ballast which ought to have been
thrown out when no longer necessary to steady him.
As a dramatist he has all the sailor's gratitude for
the friend in his hour of need, but like him, Eugene
O'Neill may discover one day that his friend was
just a shipping master, who had an understanding
with the captain to see that the crew signed on. To
leave the metaphor, whose complete implications he
will certainly understand, it may dawn upon the
author of "Anna Christie" and "The Hairy Ape"
that the æsthetes of the theater must some day deliver the goods, and it is he whom they will deliver
as proof of their genius.

One has not to talk long to Eugene O'Neill in
order to discover why he alone has projected the
seaman into literature and the theater. Even in his
present phase of life, his existence has none of the
stability, emotional, intellectual or material, befitting the foremost living American dramatist, whose
position as a man of letters is already consecrated.
Latent in him, and exploding at intervals, is a wildness that has nothing in common but externals with
the usual outburst of literary and theatrical bohemia.
Here is deep-seated revolt against restraints of all
kinds, against the humdrum of well-ordered society,
coupled with a keen consciousness of the absurdity
both of acquiescence and rebellion, a complete absence of illusion, outside the realm of art, where
illusion belongs. This is the element in O'Neill

which marks him off from all the romantic intellectuals who have written about the sea, whether of the
variety that acquires its seamanship roaming about
docks and lunching with literary mariners in port,
or that equally misleading variety, the ex-sailor,
who romanticizes his life as it recedes from him.

Eugene O'Neill has in his blood and in his imagination the roving, restless impulse which drives men
to the sea, traps them in their own weakness, tor-
tures them, and then lulls them, from time to time,
by the curious, wild poetry of the sea, which is the
will-o'-the-wisp after which they grope. These are
the men whom O'Neill describes. Outside his plays,
you will find them in the forecastle, and even at
the Captain's table, if the vessel be a tramp or a
cargo-boat, unspoiled by the compromises of the
modern liner. Men who are conservatives in rebellion, who scorn the dull monotony of the land-
man's life, yet spend their days scraping rust, caulk-
ing seams and painting funnels; shoveling and trim-
ming coal, watching the little flame in the engine-
room of an oil-burner, taking eventless watches,
worrying through countless forms and swirling red-
tape at the end of every voyage, with its dreary,
repetitious sequel of disputes, illnesses, harassing
ship chandlers and brokers, boarding-house masters,
saloon keepers, brothels; finally the consul and the
pilot, and off on the same round.

These are not the sailors beloved of the romantic
literati; they do not lean over the side, gazing into
the glowing sunset under some tropical sky, and
dream such dreams as Conrad's novels are made of.
They live in stuffy, uncomfortable quarters; those
blessed with a porthole never open it. Fresh air is

as incompatible with their habits as the uniforms which they discard at sea, because even the caps are not designed to stay on in a breeze. In their paradoxical and inexplicable world Eugene O'Neill is at home. He knows what revolts and sentimentalities are bred there, what elusive quest brings men to answer the delusive call of the sea. It is not a pretty world, but a primitive one, which has been prettified, even by realists, in the literature of seafaring. This dramatist has both seen and lived this life, but above all, his whole being is informed by the very spirit of these adventurers, so wild and feeble, so plaintive and so defiant.

That is why, in his neat blue suit with his shy smile and his sloe-black, shining eyes, Eugene O'Neill incarnates some quality which seems to be the quintessence of his work. It is the quality of wildness which understands and exults in the primitive and fundamental passions of elemental human beings. When he leaves the sea, his effort is to strip off the coverings which conceal the elemental, whether those of the Pullman car emperor or the welded married couple. In spite of his earnestness, his conscience as an artist, one feels that he is straining at the leash which attaches him to the society of the arts and their creators. He has the restless movements of one who still searches beyond the horizon. In a very special sense he "does not belong." He should not.

19. JOSEPH HERGESHEIMER

THERE are no angles in Joseph Hergesheimer. A round, chubby, bland figure, presenting a smooth surface, he is as free from shadows and half-tones as his work is free from mystery. It carries one along, as he does, by the force of exterior charm, by a child-like ingratiating quality, which does not perplex or challenge the mind, but flatters and soothes the senses. In the fullest meaning of the word, the man is sensual, that is to say, his whole physical being, all his senses, are perpetually awake and responsive to every appeal that can be made to them. No moralist has ever indicted him, his books are admitted into every family, and young girls can read him in the domestic circle around the hearth without fears for their mothers' morals, yet he is a dangerous person compared with the austere Mr. Cabell, who connotes so much wickedness; he is a complete Pagan, an instinctive hedonist. His creed is all the more subversive because he has never consciously formulated it. He is not concerned with ideas but with life.

This plump, florid, exuberant, smiling figure is the incarnation of all that asceticism would destroy; he is like a child clutching at every brightly colored, moving object that passes. He is eager for beauty, for the color and music of life; the ecstasies of renunciation have no meaning for him. He has surrounded himself with everything that he craves, for he is a child whose nursery is full of attractive playthings, gaudy, expensive playthings, designed to transport him as far away as possible from this world's sordidness and miseries. His clothes must be of the softest and best; they must be gay and luxurious. He delights in the brightness of his purest silk handkerchiefs and ties, in his flaring tweeds, in the superfine material of his dinner-jacket. His toys amuse him without end. He can play with the thought of chic hotels, elaborate drinks, fashionable clubs. The latest in reading-lamps, imported cigarettes, cigar-lighters, electric devices ensuring the maximum of lazy comfort when breakfasting in bed; the sheen of brocades and satins; the appeal of luxury, costly, useless, arrogant; the lure of beauty, precious, aggressive, triumphant—these are the stuff of Joseph Hergesheimer's dreams.

For these he is all appetite and receptivity, as he flaunts his delight and revels ingenuously in their possession. His visual imagination dominates him, and one feels that, for all his display, there is an almost impersonal artistic joy expressed, which goes far beyond the mere animal satisfaction of the successful man. Hergesheimer appreciates his success for what it can give him, as he appreciated the beauty of Linda Condon, as he publicly avowed his joy in the contemplation of Miss Lilian Gish who, better perhaps than his own symbolic doll, Cytherea, embodies the apotheosis of that to him transcendent loveliness that just is, impenitent, unproductive, extravagant, costly. The more exorbitant his toy, the deeper his response, for his devotion to beauty is absolute in precise proportion to his unreasoning, undisciplined desire for the beautiful in all its forms, from the highest to the lowest. His tactile and visual sense are so primitively keen that he evokes the color and the very touch of lovely things in a manner explicable only by reference to himself. This is not so much the art of a writer as the capacity of the man to transfer to the printed page his own tingling sensations. If the imagination which conceived the lines and designs of Persian carpetry could find a voice in this century, it would utter cries and yearnings comparable to those of Joseph Hergesheimer.

Exotic, however, he is not. The Pennsylvania Dutch solidity is here, both in the build of the man and in the assurance with which he keeps his two feet well planted on the ground and his head well beneath the clouds. His materialism is æsthetic; his realism has a mystic quality that comes from his transmutation of all material things into their element of essential beauty. One watches this rubicund face, those eyes twinkling behind enormous tortoise-shell spectacles and accentuating the impression of round-eyed, childish wonder and delight at the prospect of so many good things within reach. A popular and successful novelist, for he has the suffrages of the mass and the appreciation of the discriminating. A self-made man, whose fame has come to him by his own unaided effort. Why should he not be pleased with himself and with such others as he selects to divert his leisure? Is he not imbricated by successive layers of success and prosperity, so that he can now present the self-satisfied front of the man who has arrived?

Watch those eyes, wide-opened, inquiring. They reveal a sensitivity other than that physical capacity for receiving impressions. They are the eyes of the fat boy who was delicate and unhappy, who characteristically threw his first piece of financial good fortune into the lottery of beauty which tempted him with the prize of Italy, that most enchanting of youthful dreams. They are the eyes of the young writer who wrote and re-wrote for fourteen years before he could sell his first story, whose ill health was such that his nose bled as he leaned over his manuscripts. This side of Joseph Hergesheimer lives on beside that antithetical self which has been so fully realised. It goes with him into his study when he throws again the dice in the game which he plays with fate.

Sometimes a small number rolls up, not the high score of "Java Head," "The Three Black Pennys" or "Linda Condon." He is distressed and puzzled —that puzzled look flits across his face when he finds that all is not well in the criticism about him. His face puckers like that of a child who has been laughing and crowing, but who suddenly realizes that everybody is not satisfied with him. Criticism is still an ordeal to him, and that is perhaps the most obvious indication of what he so carefully conceals beneath his flamboyant aggressive exterior, his infinite seriousness in his art and his search for perfection. The chronicler of hotels *de luxe*, the arbiter of flashy elegance, the creator of Linda Condon, of Tao Yuen, the mystic materialist, Joseph Hergesheimer, is an artist of authentic lineage.

20. SINCLAIR LEWIS

TALL, slim and well-barbered; his sandy hair sleeked down on either side of an immaculate parting; his clothes carefully pressed; two inches of shirt cuff showing; his shoes well-shined—Sinclair Lewis looks the personification of conventional elegance, as badly dressed as only the wearer of standardized fashions for men can be, when every trace of individuality, of personal taste, is lost in a resolutely orthodox combination of "what the well-dressed man is wearing." Sartorially he realizes the ideal of the supporters of nationally advertised products, "authentic styles for the better-dressed man," "designed to combat the rigors of hot weather, and in addition, to give that lasting dressy appearance," "suits in the New York manner, smart, cool-looking, and spirited," which "excel in smartness as well as service," "tailored in accordance with our own specification" and unexcelled "in patterns, styling, and fit." He looks the part of an aggressive, forward-looking, up-standing citizen, a sales promoter of ability, a key man and live wire, who works entirely on leads and full organization support, 80 per cent of whose annual business consists of repeat orders.

His appearance does not belie his activities, for Sinclair Lewis is the drummer of ideas, the sales executive of the new American literature. He has made the Revolt of the Younger Generation a paying proposition, operating an exclusive territory on a royalty basis, and presenting an unusual household specialty, burlesque made up to look like satire. Every home a prospect; its simplicity sells it.   If you are interested in building a repeat business for the future, Mr. Sinclair Lewis can demonstrate his product; attractive book combinations that get orders; unlimited possibilities, with large royalties, selling a guaranteed product to an unlimited market, well prepared by extensive advertising.   What are you hitting at?   Have you read "Main Street" and "Babbitt," or are you just drifting along with "Tarzan of the Apes" and "Flaming Youth"? Are you reading the books for which nature has specially fitted you—the books that make you feel SUPERIOR—or are you just plugging along at the novels which the movies suggest to you?   If you feel that you have not the place in the civilized minority to which you are entitled, let our expert analyst tell you what you would look like in Gopher Praïrie.   Get rid of that Main Street feeling.

There is pep and punch in this hustling, gogetting herald of a new era in American literature. As an academic admirer has said, "Everything that is candid, fresh, alert, clean, supple, active and darting, he likes," and he has "an inclination for purposeful young men who keep themselves fit." "This enterprising young man is notably hardheaded, a hard-worker, with a good workman's prejudice in favor of keeping himself and his tools in order.   Mr. Sinclair Lewis's beauty is always tonic—never relaxing."   Inevitably criticism of him sets out to be literary but almost subconsciously drops to the level and the *clichés* of the Male Help

Wanted advertisements, the prospectuses of Correspondence Colleges and Physical Training Institutes. Criticism can deal only with what values are presented for its judgment. Sinclair Lewis inevitably suggests such compliments and appreciation as are due to his qualities as a clean-cut, energetic, attractive young business man of letters, with a line of goods that sell well, and a line of talk which captures the most unpromising "prospects." His literary technique is that of the follow-up letter, and his conversation has the charm of snappy salesmanship. He has "put over" something which is excellent parody and laughable burlesque, when taken in small doses, but which seems almost as good as authentic satire to customers bemused by his sales efficiency. It is no wonder that, while elevating him to the class of great satirists, his champions employ a language which, like his own, has none of the accents appropriate to the occasion. A Swift, a Flaubert, a Samuel Butler, are not congratulated on the exemplary practical virtues of their lives and teaching, their appeal is not measured in terms which might have validity in selecting an agent for Studebaker cars, or a bank clerk for promotion to the rank of tenth Assistant Vice-President. "Madame Bovary" was not written by a man who was crisp, darting, purposeful and fit, nor were hard-headedness and enterprise the traits which recommended Swift to the notice of his contemporaries. By their adjectives, ye shall know them, and those associated with Sinclair Lewis have little relation either to satire or to literature in general. He inspires the emotions peculiar to the kind of achievement at which he excels. His transparent honesty absolves him from the slightest suggestions of obtaining fame under false pretenses. He has put on the market a perfect substitute for the glad book, and has reaped the reward of pioneering enterprise. Have you a little Babbitt in your home?

His achievement, in the last analysis, is himself. In two lengthy self-portraits he explains his own success. His intentions are serious, and the rewards indicate how exactly the public recognized in him a man and a brother. It is the genius of salesmanship to be able to sell precisely the same article as the one it is to displace on the ground that the new one is different. It is the genius of Sinclair Lewis that he is able to combine the outlook of Carol Kennicott with the language and technique of his now famous realtor and boom the result as a satire on both. Old-fashioned manufacturers of marketable fiction are dismissed as popular entertainers, and derive whatever consolation they can from their perpetual presence at the head of best-selling lists, to offset the failure of the intellectuals to take them seriously. The author of "Main Street" shares their arithmetical glory, and his advertisements, like theirs, speak only of quantities sold and amounts of paper consumed in coping with the demand, but at the same time professors talk of his "significance," and disconsolate Liberals, always pathetically eager for an incongruous ally, hail him as another liberator breaking the shackles of conventionalism and commercialism from the limbs of the American People. The latter, with their accustomed flair, did not take long to realize that Sinclair Lewis was just gently "kidding" himself and their friends. This was no austere and superior highbrow, trying to ridicule the things they held sacred. He could burlesque as amusingly as Will Rogers, and as repetitiously, but there was more for the money—the speculators, too, always buy up the seats for the Follies, whereas his books were as readily procurable as any other nationally advertised commodity.

This, then, is "the significance of Sinclair Lewis," that he has burlesqued himself and "gotten away with it." He holds up the mirror to every face but that of the beholder, and by the supreme exercise of all the arts in the repertory of the energetic salesman, he has put over what the more timid would have deemed an unsalable product. He has done in literature what is done every day by the enterprising people whose advertisements emblazon the nightly heavens, and crowd even his own prose into a series of little segments concealed in the back pages of popular magazines. He has brought the civilized minority within the reach of all. He has persuaded the mob that it can appreciate satire, by taking the sting from its deadliest foe, for satire cannot rise above the level of the satirist. And so, this lithe, neat, well-groomed young American business man, on whose every garment and idea one can see the label that is a guarantee of authenticity, has come into his own, just like the hero of a success magazine story. He has carried the gospel of 100% Americanism into the effete countries of Europe and shown them what a live, two-fisted, literary he-man can do. In return, he has begun to take on a certain flavor of cosmopolitan experience, realizing the sweet uses to which a monocle may be put, and the charms of an established social hierarchy, where men are not merely men, but sometimes gentlemen. He has discovered, like so many of his countrymen, that it pays to advertise . . . Babbitt.

21. GEORGE BERNARD SHAW

A LONG, lanky figure with nervous, swinging gait, and the most voluminous light brown overcoat, reaching down almcst to his heels, or bellied by the wind and floating behind him like the tail of some bustling comet. He strides at a very rapid pace through the streets of this native Dublin of his, whose accent he has preserved, but which has seen little of the distinguished expatriate, George Bernard Shaw, during the forty odd years of his struggle and fame in London. He is on his way to address the first meeting of his compatriots which has ever been so honored. He does not approve of Dublin. "There is nothing more destructive," he will say, "than the sterile mockery of Dublin." He does not approve very much of Ireland, for that matter. There is too much propaganda for the Irish language and not enough for dental clinics. "I have never seen so many bad teeth as during my visit here." A hiss from the patriotic audience, protesting against such blasphemy against the sacred tongue of Kathleen ni Houlihan. Imperturbably Bernard Shaw retorts: "If you hiss me again, I'll deliver my lecture in Irish, and not one of you will understand a word of it."

When he comes on the platform, memory protests in vain against this betrayal of the legend of the tawny suit, red tie and flannel shirt of the heroic age of Fabianism. This spruce old gentleman, in a double-breasted blue serge suit looks like a re-

tired sea captain, only the amazing pallor of his
face and the small conical hands indicate that his
origins have nothing nautical about them but this
blue serge orthodoxy and meticulous neatness.
What remains, however, of the legendary G. B. S.
is the beard, now white, but still thrust derisively
at his audience to emphasize a point, as in the days
of its flamboyant redness, and those quizzical, 'animated gray-blue eyes beneath bushy eyebrows, whose
gray in no way detracts from their Mephistophelian
lift at the outer corners. As he speaks he admires
his long fingers, holding them up for inspection with
the gesture of a manicurist examining her handi-
work. He talks on the platform as he does in private, at a conversational level, entirely extempore,
and with deliberate suppression of all oratorical
effects and appeals to the emotions. He addresses
himself to the mind, and not the heart. He throws
back his head, and his eyes glitter and flash when
he makes a thrust which he judges effective.

Dublin, however, is not the place where he shines.
There are too many Dubliners as detached from
England as himself, who get no thrill of blasphemy
or wonder at his aloof analysis of the English soul,
which creates such an impression in London amongst
natural-born Britishers. His staple dish of Fabian
economics is also wasted because his Irish audience
is unfamiliar with the rudiments of that doctrine,
and is anxious only for a word on the eternal question of Ireland's wrongs. On this subject Bernard
Shaw, it seems, is exasperating, in spite of his reputation in England as a seditious Irishman. He
turns to the topic of Irish literature, since he has
actually read and met Irish authors, whereas he is

completely out of touch with the generation at work in the social and political fields. When repatriated, Bernard Shaw, the Socialist, finds the country gentry more congenial than these wild-eyed people who organize trade unions, strikes, insurrections and Free States. The atavism of the Irish Protestant gentleman is strong.

On literature, however, he has promised to speak. The scene is one of Dublin's intellectual slums, where the distinguished visitor has blundered, owing to a similarity of name between this organization and the National Literary Society, an institution of some historical pretensions, at least. The mistake has not facilitated a task already rather beyond even Bernard Shaw's power of improvisation. In the course of conversation I gently insinuate that, on this occasion, the tables are turned. *This* time he is addressing an audience which knows all about the subject, while he knows almost nothing. He looks at me disapprovingly and has no reply. On the platform his deficiencies reach the level of mere echolalia; his next sentence is suggested by the last word of what he has just said, with but the vaguest relation to the ostensible theme. The wit and paradoxes are absent. One hears, with the recognition due to a friend from copy-book days, that travel broadens the mind, that literature must be developed by the crossing of cultures, that Irish literature is negligible except for those writers who have traveled and lived abroad: James Joyce, John M. Synge, James Stephens. His repertory of names is short, and conveniently so, for it would be sad to break in upon so profound a meditation with the names of James Clarence Mangan, Sam-

uel Ferguson, Standish O'Grady, George W. Russell, Francis Ledwidge, Daniel Corkery, Seumas
O'Kelly, Padraic O'Conaire and many others, all
of whom lived and wrote in Ireland, and failed to
follow the example of Bernard Shaw.

While these thoughts naturally occur to the mind
of his humblest auditor, Shaw is admiring his nails
and aggressively proclaiming, without knowing it,
his complete ignorance of Anglo-Irish literature.
In his haste to say something that will disturb, he
soon is caught in the meandering stream of his
remarks, and is dilating, nobody knows why, on the
absurdities of those who claim that India has a literature and culture of its own. Visions of barbarians with rings in their noses begin to haunt us,
the voice of the brilliant Socialist, Fabian, playwright and paradoxer, goes on pronouncing a discourse which has the peculiar ring one would associate with the confidences of an Anglo-Indian official, retired, or home on leave, when the requisite
proportion of whisky and soda has induced in him
the usual lamentations about the "beastly natives."
It becomes my painful duty to remind the speaker
that we have heard all this sort of thing before, to
attempt, with some show of good humor, to insinuate that even intellectual slum-children do not
propose votes of thanks unless they have something
to be thankful for, to appeal to the speaker's reputation for better things, to his higher nature, so to
speak. He disapproves of this disrespectful levity;
it seems his iconoclasm does not begin at home.
Bernard Shaw does not agree with Dublin, and
Dublin does not improve Bernard Shaw. The return of the native is a qualified success.

22. G. K. CHESTERTON

IN two square, low-ceilinged rooms, whose walls are covered with portraits and pencil sketches by John Butler Yeats, a complete iconography of the Irish literary renaissance, a crowd drifts and coagulates. The artist is many miles away from this charming little house in the country, so close to Dublin, yet so rural, set amidst an expanse of open fields, with a deep blue, rounded rampart of mountains on one close horizon, and the lighter blue sea just visible on the more distant easterly line. But many of the originals of those portraits are in his daughters' house to meet Mr. Gilbert Keith Chesterton. It is the period during the war when Irish antagonism to England has flared up in a bitterness unequaled for a generation or more. A visit to Dublin had become as regular a part of the routine of war correspondents, those like H. W. Nevinson, whose life-long dream has been of peace, and those who combined propaganda amongst the unconverted neutrals with a professional delight in being present wherever life was disturbed and dangerous. G. K. Chesterton's ostensible mission may have been what it will, in practice his function as one of our conquerors was to thrash out the exhausted subject of Ireland and the World War.

Somewhat diminished in volume since the days when the list of a hansom betrayed the arrival of G. K. C. at the offices of the "Daily News" in Fleet Street, with the eleventh hour copy for his depress-

ingly sprightly articles, the English visitor sat surrounded by the angriest-looking group of normally
amiable persons which I have ever seen. These
intense, eager, straining faces, in which emotion
and intelligence dominated all the ruder faculties,
heightened the contrast with this great, burly, red-
cheeked figure of John Bullish build, whose piping
voice, with its pronounced nasal, Cockney twang,
derived a further emphasis from the prevailing soft
brogue of those about him. One murmurs Ezra
Pound's apostrophe "To a New Cake of Soap":

> Lo, how it gleams and glistens in the sun
> Like the cheeks of a Chesterton.

With a vast and cheerful innocence G. K. Chesterton had become involved in the inevitable argument, beginning, of course, quite practically with
the more or less practical question: Should Ireland
have been conscripted? And if not, why not?
Nothing afforded the political metaphysicians of the
time more bracing intellectual exercise than to debate this then burning topic with an Englishman,
and for preference, an Englishman of notoriously
liberal and pro-Irish sympathies. With a good
Tory there was neither argument nor dispute; each
understood the other perfectly; there were no half-
tones and no mysteries to be cleared up. With the
sympathetic Englishman, the situation was different. He simultaneously wanted to have his con-
scription cake, as a loyal Englishman, and to eat it
as a Liberal of principle. With the intention of
developing this position and providing the Irish
intelligentsia with their favorite sport, over a territory of which every inch had been surveyed, the

Chestertonian conversation had begun. But, needless to say, it had soon degenerated into a discussion which was reducing the audience to moans of positive mental pain.

Æ. entreated me, as a new and unexhausted arrival, to join the circle and see how long I could last without losing my mind. Gilbert Chesterton, entirely unruffled and apparently oblivious of the mental wreckage strewn about him, smiled benignly and resumed his discourse. The English and the German races it seemed were entirely unrelated, whereas France and England were natural allies. Never since her history began had Germany contributed anything to art or science; her philosophers were negligible; her music of no account; her scientific attainments mere imitation, dependent upon the inventive genius of France. It would be wrong, of course, to conscript Irishmen by legal force, but inasmuch as the Germans, as everybody knew, had impaled babies on their bayonets, mutilated women and deliberately destroyed cathedrals, like the uncouth and unchanged descendants of the Huns that they were, it was inconceivable that any Irishman of military age could refrain from joining the British army.

Interspersed with these philosophical utterances were reflections on the fundamental traits of the true-born Englishman, as a Catholic, beer-drinking, beef-eating and delightful, medieval character, the worthy citizen of "Merrie England," whose occasional lapses into a Prussianism, which, as an honest English Liberal he would not deny, were due entirely to the unfortunate presence, at a certain moment in the history of the dynasties, of German

elements. The piping voice went on, while ago-
nized murmurs of "Kant," "Beethoven," "Wag-
ner," "Cromwell," and words to that effect, rent
the air, while men turned pale with helpless rage,
and gazed in wonder at so childlike and bland a
soul. Whenever he hit upon some little paradox
or play upon words, Chesterton's huge frame would
shake and his vast chuckle would give the signal
for laughter, which did not, however, even mate-
rialize in a smile. The witticisms were as feeble
as the history, "other Casements opening on the
foam of such very perilous seas," and so forth. The
eternal Broadbent in John Bull's other Island, oh,
so genial, kind, good-humored and happy. Add to
a solid dough of aboriginal Liberalism the spice of
neo-Catholicism, a sprinkling of enthusiasm for
peasant proprietorship, and the brittle icing of
merely verbal paradox—an indigestible dish to lay
before an underfed nation, with unmistakable symp-
toms of national dyspepsia.

Close-ups

23. GEORGE JEAN NATHAN

IMPROVING upon the playwright, as is the dramatic critic's privilege, George Jean Nathan has modified Shakespeare's dictum, "all the world's a stage," restricting it to that portion of the world which is his own universe. George Nathan's world is a drawing-room comedy, which might be called "The Importance of Not Being Earnest," in which he plays the part of John Worthing; his life is a stage from which he surveys the real world as though it were a darkened auditorium filled with people whose actual preoccupations are utterly remote from those of the play in which he is perpetually engaged. He is completely absorbed in his art, his part in that comedy within whose three walls all his reality is confined. That reality is the reality of sophisticated comedy, in which an adept and skillful bachelor passes through a crisis induced by blonde tresses and sparkling wines, or is the benevolent spectator of some family tangle whose solution is effected by his friendly acquaintance with the eternal weaknesses of human nature. One thinks of him as eternally going through the gestures of arriving at his rooms, being relieved of his opera hat and cloak lined with crimson silk by an English valet, settling down in front of a fire with whiskey and soda and cigars at his elbow, and reviewing a day well misspent.

As befits the player of such parts George Jean Nathan's appearance is unreal, in the sense that he always seems to have the benefit of such illusion as footlights and the barrier of the proscenium arch confer. He has recorded his birthplace as Fort Wayne, Indiana, and his age as forty-two, while crediting Cornell University with his education. To see him, however, is to doubt these things, and to discover a subtle coquetry in the public profession of facts so utterly irreconcilable with the spectacle presented to his audience. What are the connotations of Indiana? Edward Cary Eggleston, Theodore Dreiser, Booth Tarkington, Meredith Nicholson; Hoosier schoolmasters, circuit riders, Hoosier holidays—the rough joys, the burly figures, the simple virtues of a pioneer society. What are these to Hecuba or Hecuba to them! They seem not merely remote, but incredible as the background of an existence whose natural boundaries are the Adlon Hotel in Berlin, the Hotel Ritz in the Place Vendôme, or the Cavendish in London. As difficult to imagine Cornell University the cradle of such elegances as those of which this modern Petronius is the arbiter. These imply the curious combination of a jazzed Oxford and a Heidelberg or Bonn where pedantry took the form of exhaustive researches in the theater, and the *Corpsbrüder* were members of a Borussia composed of super-men about town.

George Jean Nathan's forty-two years, however, are the supreme triumph of his art in the comedy of life, for he has that air of eternal youth which is the prerogative of theatrical stars. At a recent dinner party this youth was taken for the son of Theodore Dreiser; he is slim, dark and dapper, and looks like a preternaturally knowing college-boy, as he sits with an inevitable cigar between his teeth, a cigar whose end he never bites off in the common manner of simple men, but which he carefully snips with a gold cutter, wielded with the assurance of an Oxford man biting the stem of a pipe. His suits are always freshly pressed and although he sits down the knees of his trousers never bag, being governed by that mysterious law of the theater which used to excite the scorn of Bernard Shaw, and which inspired a realistic revolt that might have destroyed the sartorial traditions of the stage, had not Sir George Alexander and Charles Hawtrey been there to hold the line unbent against Shavian radicalism. It is not improbable that the soles of Nathan's boots are as white under the instep as those that tread the boards of drawing room comedy. He never lounges and his movements are as careful, even in moments of relaxation, as those of any actor. His pyjamas are as gaudy and unnatural as those of Sacha Guitry in *Faisons un Rêve*.

His entire wardrobe and make-up are so essential a part of him that they have been catalogued in essentials and preserved for posterity in a volume now rare but fortunately deposited in the Congressional Library. Thus, he wears an amethyst ring, a number $14\frac{1}{2}$ collar and a $7\frac{1}{4}$ hat; he owns three top hats, three suits of evening clothes and thirty-eight overcoats, ranging from "heavy Russian fur to the flimsiest homespun," to quote the programme

notes, and "one with an alpine hood attachment."
All his clothes are made to his order, including his
hats, and he has a seductive array of walking-sticks,
fourteen in number. His apartment has been designed obviously for scenic effect rather than comfort or permanent habitation. The heavily cur-
tained windows do not open, and one suspects that,
if they did, they would look into the wings of a
theater; the bookshelves have the unconvincing air
of stage properties, but the divans, cushions, shaded
lights and various elegant devices for the holding,
passing around and consumption of alcoholic liquors
are clearly intended for effective use in some of his
important scenes. If he has not installed the contraption for the production of artificial rain outside
those closed windows, which he described with such
enthusiasm a while ago, it is because this is not in
the cosmic script from which he learns his lines.
Whenever rain is required the stage carpenters will
see to it that Mr. Nathan's act is not spoiled.

In the circumstances, it is not unnatural that his
indifference to the ordinary affairs of the world is
notorious. To expect him to be aware of coal-
strikes, wars, transit commissions or the Federal
Reserve system would be to expect a performance
of "The Merchant of Venice" to be interrupted because Mr. Walter Hampden was reminded by the
text that he should say something about the proportion of Jews at Harvard. Such echoes of matters outside the lines of the comedy in which he
performs as reach his ears are only such as might
be mentioned in the dressing-room between the acts.
He has heard of prohibition, but does not believe
it, and the only social problem on which he has ex-

pressed himself with feeling is that of trade union-
ism for actors. His confession of faith is specific
and revelatory:

"What interests me in life . . . is the surface
of life": life's music and color, its charm and ease,
its humor and its loveliness. The great problems
of the world—social, political, economic and theological—do not concern me in the slightest. . . .
If all the Armenians were to be killed to-morrow
and if half of Russia were to starve to death the
day after, it would not matter to me in the least.
What concerns me alone is myself and the interests
of a few close friends. . . . On that day during the
World War when the most critical battle was being
fought, I sat in my still, sunlit, cozy library com-
posing a chapter on æsthetics for a new book on the
drama. And at five o'clock, my day's work done,
I shook and drank a half dozen excellent apéritifs."

Allowing that the "sunlight" mentioned in the
closing sentence is a theatrical convention, how perfectly the scene is set for George Jean Nathan's
comedy of living. It must not be forgotten that
this man is no mime, no actor in stage plays, that
he confesses a marked dislike for the society of the
professional actor. His desire is for those "few
close friends" who share with him the program
in a more refined and subtle play than any he is
called upon to discuss in his professional capacity.
His business is the theater, and his business is
his pleasure, but of life itself he has made a play
in which he is the leading character. And thus he
has contrived his existence so as to shut out of it
every element which might clash with the charming
make believe of the theater. He touches the stage

at all points but the routine of the humdrum world
at none. When this pure æsthete is compelled to
listen to the conversations of Mencken he assumes
that slightly distressed and bewildered air which
most of us had as children when we were taken out
of the theater into the streets, the glare of the footlights still in our eyes, the glamor of impossible
landscapes and gaudily beautiful women contrasting with the sordid aspects of the city about us.
Nathan is interested in Beauty, especially if it be
small and blonde, while Mencken's mind ceaselessly
revolves in the vortex of insoluble social problems,
political chicaneries and the endless circle of human
folly. Ziegfeld's Follies are a more engaging spectacle in the eyes of his colleague.

When Charles Lamb argued that the Restoration
dramatists must not be damned as immoral because
the society they described was fictitious, a convention not to be measured by normal standards, he
adopted an attitude which must be adapted by those
who would appreciate George Jean Nathan. His
confessions would indicate him as a monstrosity, as
an inhuman and intolerable person. But the truth
is he is a highly entertaining and pleasant fellow,
whose very hypochondria is not distressing, even
when it takes the strange form of perpetually plugging his nostrils with pink cotton over which some
medicinal incantation has been pronounced, or of
unceasingly inhaling a tube of menthol—these
being apparently his chief winter sports. The clew
to the enigma is the fact, which cannot be too frequently emphasized, that all his world is a comedy,
a stage, upon which the eruption of naïve spectators
would be as unseemly as the hooting of the villain

in a melodrama by untutored rustics righteously indignant on behalf of an outraged and harried heroine. When John Worthing appears in mourning for the imaginary Ernest of Wilde's play, one does not protest against this misuse of the habiliments of grief. The scene is one of the most amusing in the three diverting acts of "The Importance of Being Earnest." It would certainly be disingenuous to the point of complete ingenuousness to forget where Nathan was and to make him step out of his part.

In George Nathan, then, we have the perfect dramatic critic, the archetype, the *Kritiker an sich*, as Kant might say. He is the complete man of the theater, his mind is as uncontaminated with irrelevancies as that of a politician with ideas or that of a professional moralist with a sense of decency or fair play. Everything human is alien to him unless it concerns the theater, of which his lore is profound and extensive and of which he never tires. Of the thirteen volumes which stand to his credit, two are plays, six are specifically devoted to the drama, and the character of the remaining five is well summed up in the title of one of them "The World in Falseface." That, after all, *is* his world, whether he be in New York, London or Vienna; whether his topic be Sam Bernard or Eleonora Duse, Ann Pennington and Bert Savoy or Ibsen and Synge. When he writes his impressions of travel he is really drawing attention to the sets for his comedy. For example:

"The Malecon at two o'clock of a late Spring morning, with its tiara of amber lights, the harbor of Havana playing its soft lullaby against the sea-wall, and Morro Castle blinking like a patient owl across the waters; the garden of the Hôtel de France et d'Angleterre at Fontainebleau in the twilight, with the cannon of the French artillery in the late summer maneuvers echoing dully in the outlying forests; Hampton Court on a lazy afternoon in the late autumn of the year, deserted, still, with the leaves falling across the withered flower-beds and up from the Thames, the sound of a lonely paddle; mid-winter dawn in the Siegesallee of Berlin; the steps of the Tcheragan Serai in Constantinople on a moonlit night trembling in the mirror of the Bosporus; the palm-bordered road out of Hamilton, Bermuda, on a rainy day in May, with the smell of the sea dripping from the great leaves; the hurricane deck of a ship gliding noiselessly through the blue star-shot cyclorama of a Caribbean night, with the intermittent click of poker chips from the smoking-room and the orchestra below playing the waltz song from 'Sari'; the Kärntner-Ring of Vienna just after eleven of a November evening, with its elaborately costumed police, and the hackmen bawling for fares, and the young girls selling Kaiserblumen, and the crowds in dominoes of a dozen colors on their way to the flower ball, and cavalrymen kissing their sweethearts in the middle of the street; the path of pines that winds up the hill on the far side of Lake Mohegan, its carpet of moss still damp from the retreat of April, an hour from Times Square. . . ."

The scenery, it will be noticed, is not in the expressionistic or Dadaist style. George Jean Nathan does not see life in the flickering tempo of a Walter Hasenclever; he sees it very steadily, but never whole. In his critical capacity he has fewer limitations than any other dramatic critic to-day and can enjoy "Krausmeyer's Alley" as much as "Anna Christie"; Rostand's conventional romanticism holds him but does not detract from his enjoyment of "Rosmersholm" or "Man and Superman." He welcomed the Irish Players in "The Whiteheaded Boy" when most of his American colleagues were supercilious, but he joined them in praise of "The Miracle" and the Moscow Art Theatre. When one remembers the catholicity of his tastes it would seem as if he must have devoted his years of criticism to an amiable acquiescence in whatever happened to be fashionable, but his record is one of the harshest censure, involving him in conflicts with personages accustomed to deference or at least discreet silence. He is a singing captive in his profession, for he cheerfully attends the opening performances of plays which, on the face of it, could not interest him and are probably worthless, as he gayly demolishes the plays of friends, ignoring the polite conventions for the sake of freedom of opinion. He is as enthusiastic and full of gusto when he holds up Zoë Akins to ridicule as when he first greeted her as the author of "Papa."

His destructive efforts are more frequently remembered, although he has championed many a lost play, and might be satisfied alone by his immediate recognition of Eugene O'Neill. As might be expected, he denies the existence of constructive criticism, in the sense that it is clearly useless to point out how a play should have been written, except as a satisfaction to oneself. The author does not and cannot, as a rule, profit by the suggestions. On the famous occasion when he re-wrote a play by Augustus Thomas, simply reversing the order of the scenes, and showing that it might just as well begin at the end and work back to the beginning—the criticism was constructive, but he had no reason to believe he was doing more than amusing himself. He has a pleasant habit of divulging the obscure linguistic origins of plays which have been accepted as translations from the more familiar French, German or Spanish. This helpful pedantry has by no means established his reputation for learning, because his style is not so genteel as that of the late William Winter. Hazlitt's name never occurs in his essays unless written without a capital and used as a generic term for theatrical journalists. It would be rash to conclude from this that Nathan has never read him.

George Jean Nathan is the American counterpart of the Englishman A. B. Walkley. Two dissimilar men in every respect save their common profession of complete worldliness and their insatiable joy in the theater. Walkley takes the same pleasure in parading his French and his classical education as Nathan in concealing his omnivorous consumption of dramatic literature, and in exhibiting his apparently boundless knowledge of acted plays. The mere journalists loathe him and suspect him when many consonanted Hungarian names appear to upset their statements that a given play actually first seen in Buda Pesth, is full of the glamor of Spain. The young intellectuals apply to him their usual naïve test, namely, the absence of any display of class-room learning, and conclude that he is just a super-lowbrow. If he would only quote Aristotle and remark: "I have just been re-reading Vanbrugh"—when it is obvious that the reading is an initiation through the kind offices of some professor—if he would even write highly anti-syntactical but arty prose, they would declare, as they do of Paul Rosenfeld, he is "an important gift to critical American literature." Happily, George Jean Nathan does none of these things.

When he becomes unintelligible he does it as a gentleman gets drunk, without becoming objectionable. He never forgets his part in that quintessential comedy which is his existence. Thus he can say of his one passion, the theater: "I do not take it very seriously . . . nor . . . do I take it too lightly, for one who takes nothing very seriously takes nothing too lightly. I take it simply as, night in and night out, it comes before my eyes: a painted toy with something of true gold inside it."

CURTAIN

24. THOMAS BEER

ON first seeing Thomas Beer one becomes the victim of a strange but symbolical mirage. It seems as if one were transported back into "the fabulous forties" and were looking at a dignified dandy of the period. The auburn side-whiskers are there, and the hallucinated eye beholds a high black stock, a ruffled shirt front, a plum-colored jacket and pantaloons strapped under boots with elastic sides. From his fob hangs a bunch of seals and in his right hand he carried a tall, black-ebony cane with a gold knob. He bows ceremoniously, and with early Victorian decorum engages in the politest of polite conversation. If a lady were to faint one can see him stooping solicitously to tender smelling-salts, his gaze chastely averted, should the inevitable ceremony of unlacing her stays be performed. It is natural for him to sit on at the mahogany, after the ladies have retired to the drawing-room, to enjoy with the men the wines for which he has a cunning taste, and the modern habit of co-educational drinking seems somehow to be a violation of his instinctive pruderies. If he were ordered to go into the garden to smoke, he would acquiesce, as was the habit of his period. In the society of women he feels that a certain formality is desirable and thus he stands around stiffly making small talk when the gentlemen have rejoined what his contemporaries used to call the Sex. None the less, a monstrous fine fellow, egad!

Such is the aura which surrounds this figure
strayed into a period which will be proud to claim
his works, for all their indifference to current interests and tendencies. The man himself has been
described as resembling Henry James in the days
of his youth, but Thomas Beer has been fashioned
out of clay that presents a stronger, a more masculine outline than the capon-like flabbiness of that
eminent spinster of letters. A short, broad-shoul-
dered frame on which is set a powerful head; out
of the intense pallor of the face brown eyes with
twinkling shafts of light contemplate the scene
with quizzical humor; a determined chin and jaw
which strive subconsciously to assert themselves
against the pressure of an imaginary stock, and are
thus thrust forward from time to time with aggressive motion. A certain stiffness of movement and
formality of address are intimations of that earlier
incarnation of his, and his drawling speech corre-
sponds to a real or simulated detachment from the
life of his time. He always professes to have enjoyed the part rather than the whole, and his de-
preciatory adverbs and adjectives frequently usher
in words intended for praise. His imagination is
visual; thus his favorite expression when he wishes
to introduce a scene in which he was concerned is
the abrupt formula: spectacle (pronounced in the
French manner) of . . . then follows a sardonic
picture of some English literary giant haggling for
American dollars before condescending to the Transatlantic foreigner, the florid drawing-room and appropriately dull company of a *nouveau riche*, or
the alcoholic mazes and gyrations of a late party.
He has a historical sense of dates, which he always

mentions with the preliminary, "in the year of
grace." His profound *ennui* frequently takes refuge
in "etcetera, etcetera" (also articulated after the
French), whereby he sums up all that he might have
added to his narrative. He is distinctly bored, it
would appear, and he cannot refrain from standing
constantly with arms outstretched, in the attitude
of one who is crucified on his own boredom.

In spite of his legal training, there is nothing of
the jurist about him, but his experiences in France
with the 87th Division have left their imprint on
his mind. He insinuates, with that self-depreciat-
ing humor of his, which is one of his most endearing
traits, that the uniform of a first lieutenant did not
render him as irresistible as tradition supposes the
trappings of war should do. He would rather exchange his business suit for the flowing cape, the
cane and the dandiacal accoutrements of the early
years of this century. Khaki had no lure for him,
but he was resolved to get into the American Ex-
peditionary Force, in spite of all rebuffs, and he
did so. His view of that great adventure corre-
sponds neither to the energy he displayed in achieving his purpose, nor to the post bellum tradition of
disillusionment. The heights of patriotic rhetoric
are as alien to Thomas Beer as the depths of disgruntled radicalism. He maintains an air of disrespectful aloofness which is friendly to no party
and the enemy of none. He seems to have been
uninterested in either Germans or Allies, but intensely diverted and irritated by the contemplation
of human grandeur and imbecility in a concentrated
and panoramic form. Innumerable spectacles and
etceteras (*à la française*) punctuate his account of

military life, followed by vivid evocations of official
stupidity, masculine endurance, the eternal femi-
ninity of gallant women, and the marvelous phantasmagoria of a Europe just dragged back from the
edge of an abyss. On the whole, Thomas Beer was
rather bored by the war, but found it amusing in
spots.

As befits a man of such detachment he prefers to
dwell in a monument of Mid-Victorian architecture
within reasonable, but not too reasonable, distance
of Manhattan. In a turret of this imposing struc-
ture is the room in which he works, above the bustle
of domestic life below, its magic casements opening out on the waters of the Hudson, if not on
fairy seas forlorn. To Yonkers he retreats much
as Queen Victoria retired to Windsor Castle or
Holyrood when the festivities of London became
too much for her. Women have turned pale and
strong men have been dismayed when his native
resolution has caused him to make that pilgrimage
in the crepuscular hours before dawn, when a room
at the Club, the host's spare bedroom, or even a
shake-down on the sofa, appeals to the errant soul
of a ·softer generation. These nocturnal expedi-
tions, like the New York subways, may be intensely
uncomfortable, but there are no accidents. Thomas
Beer never fails to reach his haven, where he remains in seclusion until the still small voice of his
social conscience is heard over the telephone announcing his impending arrival in town.

Notwithstanding this agoraphobia, this aversion
for too many crowded hours of crowded city life,
he has no predilection for the country. When circumstances compel him to take up his summer resi-

dence on the island of Nantucket he is unmoved by
the sight of the soundless Atlantic which rolls in at
the very feet of his villa. He occasionally displays
a vague interest in the more ingenuous exhibitions
of Siasconset's naïve bathing beach, but the golf-
course knows him not, and he has never been known
to walk further along the cliffs than is required to
call at the post office, or visit the older colony of
visitors. For the man has a characteristic affection
for what is mature and settled; he eschews the restlessness of youth. His discourse is rarely of women,
but when a note of admiration and enthusiasm is
heard it is always in praise of the ripe charms of
some opulent matron, or the beautiful old age of a
grandmother who in her day turned the heads of all
the young bloods. He will eagerly turn to such,
away from the entreating or wondering glances of
the modern girl. If she would only hide her
shapely silken legs beneath a crinoline, and assume
the virtue of maidenly modesty, she might cause
Thomas Beer to forswear his allegiance to the past.
When confronted with the young women of the
Jazz Age his motto is: *oderint, dum metuant.* He
would rather they disliked than loved him, but perhaps he maintains a skeptical hope that some middle
course may prove possible, though he sees little to
justify that belief. We live in an incautious and
forthright age where such matters are concerned.

It is significant that Thomas Beer's first book,
"The Fair Rewards," although it carried its story
up to yesterday, was essentially a story of the past.
The life of Mark Walling lies between the period
when "The Prisoner of Zenda" was first produced
at the Lyceum Theatre and the opening of Sem

Benelli's "The Jest" at the Plymouth. It is the first stage in the author's procession backwards through the years that separate him from the epoch in which his own avatar took shape. A slender fable, it is true, but held up by a style already personal, if not yet fully evolved: "After dark Broadway was tolerable! Then the revolving people were shapes of no consequence and, with a little mist, these lights were aqueous, flotillas of shimmering points on a hovering, uncertain vastness. Now, the roadway was a dappled smear of bodies wheeled and bodies shod. The sidewalks writhed, unseemly." Here are undertones of the harmonies to be developed in "Stephen Crane: A Study in American Letters," which has given Beer a definite place in our contemporary literature.

He has used Crane as a pretext for creeping back another decade or two, and it is with obvious verve that he allows himself to revel in the period of the 'Eighties and early 'Nineties. As a literary biography the book is unique, and more would have been heard of it in the women's clubs had its author won his victories on the playing fields of Eton. But, without any taint of Teutonic or Mediterranean heresy, he is the very opposite of an Anglomaniac. "An American writer," he says, "is safest abroad when he has somewhere left in storage his entire critical sense and has for the voyage replaced it by an emotional willingness comparable to the felicity of a noticed puppy. He may then roam in his destined character, giving neither pleasure nor offense to men who will accept his admirations and hear his raptures as mature women accept the flowers and phrases of some harmless schoolboy."

Here shows that streak of irony which gives a special savor to his conversation. The sentence, too, is an illustration of a state of mind which preserves Beer from the excesses of enthusiasm or indignation, between which the average American usually oscillates when abroad.

"Stephen Crane" is, within certain limits, a complete expression of his literary personality. It is written in the manner of his own conversation, minus the spectacles and etceteras. His apparently inappropriate but actually expressive adjectives stand out effectively: "a drawing room that glowed, by night, under the jets of a *monstrous* chandelier," "this *polychromatic* paradise," "a boudoir of *shrieking* velvets and enamels," "the *gelatinous* grandees of New York," "Loti's *wailing* grace," the Bowery "a *glamorous* sink, with an *honest* average of three saloons to the block," "*laborious* prostitutes strolled from sunset to dawn on selected beats." The orotund accent of Beer's social commentary is clearly discernible in this description of Henry James: "He was so kind. From the sacred fount of his self-adoration there yet welled on gifted folks those pools of tender correspondence and those courtesies a trifle tedious, one hears, but rendered with such grace. . . . He was no longer a man. Henry James was a colored and complicated ritual that demanded of spectators a reverence unfailingly accorded. People who swooned under the burden of his final method, sat and sat in pleasure while that astonishing egotism bared in slow phrases its detached and charming appreciation of its own singular skill. . . . Critics mired themselves in verbal anguish over his successive novels. This plain and limited old bachelor commanded the world to respect him, and the world obeyed. He was so kind. . . . This master of groomed circumstance had found out a sunny garden where poisons blew as perfumes too heavy for a refined sense, and crime were shadows, not clouds, that swept across his shaved and watered turf." Such is the quintessence of his style.

Spectacle, as he would say, of Thomas Beer lounging stiffly, with arms uplifted in a crucified attitude, and discoursing of men and manners, of books and persons. From his pocket there protrudes a huge box of monstrously fat cigarettes which he consumes incessantly, at his elbow on the mantelpiece, against which he loves to recline, stands a tall Tom Collins. When some indecorous remark is interjected he clutches his face and hides his expression with tragic hands. He moves with the ponderous gravity of an Oriental deity, but the talk that drawls from that humorous mouth has all the deliberate charm that is apparent in his "Stephen Crane." He has composed for himself an attitude towards life, and his style is now a reflection of that attitude. Whether his theme be the unconscious humors of camp life in the South, the garish joys of Rosie Lewis's Cavendish Hotel, the problem of making an impecunious British author feel at home at the Maison Basque, the devious and tortuous process of procuring a preface from Conrad, or the grandeur and decadence of "the mauve decade," Beer's talk has an identical and singular charm.

In "Sandoval," his new novel, he has escaped back to New York of the period just after the Civil

War, with Dobbs Ferry as its social center, and Thor Gaar, another incarnation of the author's atavistic yearning for the light of other days. Its publication will shortly reveal the immense stride that Beer has made since he wrote "The Fair Rewards." The man and his manner have clearly emerged from the mannerism, and a real literary personality is the result, a personality which is stamped as clearly upon his life of Stephen Crane as if it were his own story. Dandies as men of letters were a phenomenon of the late eighteenth and nineteenth centuries, but D'Orsay and Brummel, and Barbey d'Aurevilly and Byron earned the first title primarily because of their clothes, which were not always mirrored in their style. With Beer the process is reversed; it is as a man of letters that he is a dandy, for his literary and intellectual personality is cultivated, ornate, elaborate and altogether striking, dandiacal in a word. And so it always evokes that shadowy aura of an insolent and formal young man, with high black stock, ruffled shirt front, a plum-colored jacket and pantaloons strapped under boots with elastic sides. From his fob hangs a bunch of seals, and in his right hand he carries a tall ebony cane with a gold knob . . . the sartorial ghost of his former self.

25. F. SCOTT FITZGERALD

NATURE has so well succeeded in imitating art that Scott Fitzgerald is a character out of his own fiction, and his life a series of chapters out of his own novels. Zelda Fitzgerald is the blonde flapper and her husband the blonde philosopher of the Jazz Age, such incarnations as only imitative Nature can produce when the models have been well set. Even physically they are such perfect types that, were their photographs to be used as illustrations to his writings, we should complain that the illustrator was lacking in originality and had contented himself with a convention. This slim, fair, blue-eyed, handsome youth, with a smile so winning that only the *clichés* of romantic fiction can describe it, with a doll-like, feminine replica of himself in his wife, and a child clearly intended to complete a moving picture of young happiness in the last scene of a novel or a film—that these three stereotyped figures out of popular magazine literature should exist in the flesh is as startling as their incongruity in the new fiction of which Scott Fitzgerald was the portent.

He wrote the literature of which he is the incarnation, and Nature adapted herself accordingly, but with pleasant irony preserved the mold from which had been cast the heroes and heroines of Harold Bell Wright. And so, with the impunity of their years, they can realize to the full all that the Jazz Age has to offer, yet appear as fresh and innocent and unspoiled as characters in the idyllic world of pure romance. The wicked uncle, Success, has tried to lead these Babes in the Wood away and lose them, but they are always found peacefully sleeping in each other's arms. The kind fairies have watched over them, as they wandered in the city underwoods, from Palais Royal to Plantation, from Rendez-vous to Club Gallant, with many a *détour* before the delayed and ever-miraculous departure for Great Neck, and safe arrival there in the most autonomous automobile on Long Island.

There are people who knew Scott Fitzgerald at Princeton, and others who meet him only at his home in Great Neck. There are even fabulous and frightened friends whose astonishment dispenses with the explanation that they knew him in St. Paul. But to meet him thus is to lose much of the comedy and drama which depend upon the scene being staged in a proper setting. The inherent fitness of things demands that he shall be seen and heard within the boundaries of Broadway's Roaring Forties, or perhaps in those Harlem cabarets dedicated to the theory that East is West and West is East and somehow the twain must meet. Music by George Gershwin, under the baton and rhythmically swinging foot of Paul Whiteman; wines and spirits by special arrangement with the Revenue Department. The autonomous car is moored somewhere near the Plaza Hotel, and, until the harsh light of dawn, the night is as young as our host, who sits with his cellarer and confidential adviser on his right, some probably intimidated and indignant friends from the hinterland on his left, and around the table such convivial persons as may happen by right of prior acquaintance, or the mellow familiarity of the hour, to be making an evening of it.

The cup-bearer, though brachycephalic and an alien, is faithful after his fashion, and under cover of his native tongue will confide his distress at the exigencies of his client, and vow his honest purpose of supplying only the best. With the craft of the race that produced Machiavelli, he tries to defeat the mechanical gesture of the hand raising a glass, by concealing highballs that have become superfluous, and by allowing the deformed receptacles of domestic Haig and Haig which have not been broached to disappear mysteriously and irrevocably under the table. Like his renowned forbear, he has devised an unwritten manual on the education of Princes, which serves its purpose as effectively as did the rules of conduct laid down by the great Florentine. One listens distractedly to the cares of this man's high office, while Scott Fitzgerald combines the most intellectual discussion with all the superficial appearances of the wildest conviviality. To the distant onlooker he must look like a college boy, celebrating. In fact, his topics may be of vast importance, even if interrupted by snatches of song or cheerful horseplay.

The truth is, Scott Fitzgerald is intensely preoccupied with the eternal verities and the insoluble problems of this world. To discuss them while waiting for supper with Miss Gilda Gray is his privilege and his weakness; the fact must not be allowed to detract from the earnestness of his queries nor the shrewdness of his views. He is one of the few frivolous people with whom one can be sure of having a serious conversation. It might almost be said that he alone makes such conversation possible in New York, where people with nothing to say specialize in profound commentary, while those with personal ideas prefer to clothe them in such a disguise as to defy casual scrutiny. Scott Fitzgerald has the responsibilities as well as the frivolities of his years. He has not yet reached the age of assent. In his moments of relaxation he becomes aware that, as the optimists say, mankind is slowly approaching by imperceptible degrees an ideal which it can never reach. The thought, very naturally, depresses him, and he turns an innocent blue eye towards the inverted bowl of heaven, and appeals for help in elucidating the problem.

In mundane matters, too, he is an exemplary citizen, whose opinions would surprise those who regard him as the personification of all the reprehensible tendencies of the new generation. Under the strongest provocation, he never hearkens to what is euphemistically known as the voice of Spring, and the unconcealed admiration of a pretty young woman, even when accompanied by the primeval rhythms of the earthiest jazz, does not tempt him from his intellectual austerity. Upon the theme of marital fidelity his eloquence has moved me to tears, and his stern condemnation of the *mores* of bohemia would almost persuade a radical to become monogamous. There are still venial and mortal sins in his calendar, and the ancestral voices of the Geraldines, speaking out of a Celtic twilight, are heard like an undertone throughout his meditations. Where so many others are conscious only of sex, he is conscious of the soul. His Catholic heaven is not so far away that he can be misled into mistaking the shoddy dream of a radical millennium as a substitute for Paradise. The contemporary goddesses of Reason seem to him ill adapted to restore the pagan rites of Venus. His confessions, if he ever writes any, will make the reader envy his transgressions, for they will be permeated by the conviction of sin, which is so much happier than the conviction that the way to Utopia is paved with adultery.

His sense of reverence is one that must endear him to people of taste, for it is apparently restricted to creators in the arts whose claims rest not upon venerable antiquity nor upon impudent modernity. Neither the iconoclasts nor the worshipers of idols can count Scott Fitzgerald as an ally. He has so admirable and complete a grasp of realities that his comments upon people and events, his estimates of character, show an almost complete absence of self-illusion. His capacity for hero-worship, nevertheless, is authentic and, at times, amusing, because so rarely misplaced. We had often discussed the work of Theodore Dreiser, for whom he confessed a respect unusual in his generation, which imagines that to treat an amusing *farceur* like Guillaume Apollinaire with the profoundest solemnity is a proof of intellectual emancipation. When he heard one day that a few people were meeting that evening at Dreiser's, he formed the heroic resolution to come and introduce himself. As we all sat in a large semicircle, gazing with disconsolate incredulity at a table covered with bottles of near-beer, a tap was heard on the door, and a moment later the dazed figure of Scott Fitzgerald appeared. Preparatory to going over the top in this manner, he had fortified himself against acts of God and the King's enemies, and had thoughtfully procured more of the same as a tribute to the dean of modern American fiction. Bearing his gifts, he penetrated the ring of strange faces, and breathlessly conveyed his homage and his parcel. After a gallant effort to engage Dreiser in literary discussion, he retreated to a seat near his overcoat and proceeded to extract from the pocket of this garment a substitute for the intoxication of the mind which he had anticipated. It was an affecting picture of the Master with the youngest of his disciples, and a testimony to the survival in Scott Fitzgerald of respect for honorable achievement, under difficulties certainly unknown to him or his contemporaries.

This poor little rich boy has taken the public into his confidence and explained how utterly impossible it was for him to make both ends meet on an annual income of $36,000. His budget as set out by him in "The Saturday Evening Post" is as elusive a document as the calculations of the astrologers who have regaled us with the totals of German reparations, upon which so many things, it would seem, depend. It would be indiscreet to suggest that the total disappearance of $12,000, which he pursues in vain through his budget, may not be entirely unrelated to the fact that no mention is made, under the head of "Charities," to his contributions to the dividends of Scottish distillers and the resurgent industries of Rheims. Nor does he take into account his embarrassing habit of using his check-book for the writing of inexplicable autographs in the tragic moments immediately preceding his flight through the

weary wastes of Long Island. Irate head-waiters
have to be mollified, it is true, and the diligence of
Broadway entertainers must be rewarded. But I
believe many of these autographs must be given out
of some subconscious thought of the certain risks of
the impending jump from the Plaza to the Fifty-
ninth Street Bridge and thence into the unknown.

As in the early days of aviation, daring passengers may take this trip, provided they have made
their last will and testament and waive all claims
to compensation in case of accident. A form of
traveler's insurance policy should be provided in
advance, and it is advisable to rehearse carefully the
Rules for Guests at the Fitzgerald house. "Visitors
may park their cars and children in the garage."
"Visitors are requested not to break down doors in
search of liquor, even when authorized to do so by
the host and hostess." "Week-end guests are respectfully notified that invitations to stay on over
Monday, issued by the host and hostess during the
small hours of Sunday morning, must not be taken
seriously." The regulations cover so many con-
tingencies that, were copies available, further comment would be useless.

By an apparently magic, and certainly unexpected, turn of the hand, the car, whose nose points
towards Columbus Circle, wheels abruptly round
to the East, dislodging various friends who have
been chatting confidently to the occupants, their
feet resting on the stepboard. Before they have
picked themselves out of the dust, nothing is visible
but the sinister gleam of the red tail-light, disap-
pearing in the pale glow of dawn. In the course of
this "raid," as the French insist on calling such

things, many adventures may befall the intrepid passengers. With all the familiar landmarks obliterated by snow and the evening festivities, when it is a moral certainty that one is miles off the true course, Scott Fitzgerald may suddenly descend from his seat at the steering-wheel and with a gracious bow invite some one who has never driven a car to steer the sleeping party to its destination. After the question of his inability to drive another yard has been adequately considered, he very cheerfully returns to his place, and, after consultation at intervals with policemen obviously insensible to the appeals of Volstead but not to those of the United States Treasury, he guides the car graciously up to his front door.

Postponing as long as possible the dawn of another day, the guests descend towards noon; they breakfast, and then speculate upon the possible intentions of the host and hostess, still lost in the sweet sleep of childhood, a spectacle to bring a tremor to the most cynical lip. A butler, since relieved of his duties, apparently understands the situation, and moves about with something of that ominous, furtive air, peculiar to majordomos in mystery melodramas. Breakfast seems to be, in Gallic idiom, the youngest of his cares. His preparations are all souvenirs of the night before. In more philosophic mood than ever Scott Fitzgerald finally appears, prepared to devote the afternoon to discussions of art and literature. When lunch has been disposed of, and the butler's reiterated invitations to his master to eat, drink and be merry have had their effect, the talk becomes animated.

In his conception of himself and his work Scott

Fitzgerald is a realist. He is under no illusions as to the difference between earning an income and earning one's laurels. He is too clever to deceive himself about inferior work, however lucrative, and he has the real literary craftsman's pride in good workmanship, and a high sense of the art of writing. His seriousness is of the kind which one respects, for it is not the seriousness so common in certain circles, with which predestined tenth-raters mask their ignorance and their total absence of all humor and proportion. It becomes evident that one may have a genuine feeling for literature and a developed sense of values without confining one's prose to the esoteric magazines. Probably Scott Fitzgerald is the one young author in America of talent who has never contributed to the sort of reviews which make compromises with every taste except that of the public. His associates have not hitherto been the geniuses who print their poems in horizontal monosyllables. Whether he can go to that Parisian bourne from which so few American literary travelers return unspoiled, remains to be seen. Evil Transatlantic communications corrupt good American literary manners.

It would be outrageous to take leave of so genial and charming a friend on this note of apprehension. If the topic were debated at Great Neck, it would not degenerate into undue solemnity. The hovering butler, for one thing, would have seen to it that Scott Fitzgerald was reminded of the amiable weaknesses of the flesh rather than those of the spirit. The certain sequel, provided one could escape the ceaseless stream of visitors, would be a drive in that adventurous car, with talk of men—

not women—and books. A call or two upon the theatrical aristocracy of the neighborhood, perhaps some silent intercourse with the taciturn Ring Lardner. The evening mood gradually envelops Scott Fitzgerald; a party must be arranged. By the time dinner is over, the nostalgia of town is upon us once more. Zelda will drive the car. We are still this side of paradise.

26. GEORGE MOORE

GEORGE MOORE is essentially an indiscretionist, who has conducted not only his education in public, as Oscar Wilde remarked, but also his private life. His Aubusson carpet and his Manets have been described endlessly, by himself and his visitors; we are as familiar with the beauty spots of his mythical mistresses, as with his belated discoveries in literature—his quaint theory that Thomas Hardy is a bad novelist, his last minute conversion to the dubious claims of Stevenson, his untenable doctrine of the incompatibility of Catholicism and literature. The living victims of his indiscretions occasionally hit back effectively, as when W. B. Yeats said to me, with a sweet smile: "What a pity Moore never had a love affair with a *lady*—always with women of his own class!" But in the presence of this wild-mannered, rubicund, malicious little gentleman, whose sole preoccupation is his craft as a writer, the legendary amorist fades from sight. One is interested in the spectacle of a man whose entire energies are concentrated upon the business of literature, who labors in the manner of a Flaubert, indefatigably pursuing the turns and phrases which afterwards read as though no effort had gone into their making. The real Moore is the hard-working, conscientious, tireless literary artist, who set out upon his career as a realist, but achieved fame as a stylist. The myth is the brilliant conversation-

alist and lover, who has served as a stalking-horse
to deceive the public, while George Moore himself
toiled steadily towards his goal, which was to endow
the literature of his time with perfect prose narrative. That myth dates right back to the origins of
his literary life, far beyond the point in "Memoirs
of My Dead Life," where his chronology begins
for so many modern readers.

One remembers the story of the wooing of Doris,
of the preliminary encounters, the advancing and
retreating, until finally the lovers set out from Marseilles to Orelay, "a moral town!—high beds and
nightshirts." It is a charming episode, but the hero
is already a character, not out of life but out of
fiction. He first strutted in George Moore's imagination more than thirty years ago. This is how he
appeared in "Confessions of a Young Man": "A
Japanese dressing gown, the ideality of whose tissue
delights me, some fresh honey and milk set by this
couch hung with royal fringes; and, having partaken
of this odorous refreshment, I call to Jack, my great
python that is crawling about after a two months'
fast. I tie up a guinea pig to the *tabouret*, pure
Louis XV; the little beast struggles and squeaks,
the snake, his black bead-like eyes are fixed, how
superb are the oscillations . . . now he strikes, and
slowly and with what exquisite gourmandise he
lubricates and swallows."

Nowadays that reads rather like a stage direction
for some motion picture of Sin, with Theda Bara
voluptuously reclining beneath the gaze of a vigi-
lant camera-man in California, or thereabouts.
Yet, it is the first sketch of the mythical George
Moore, and "Confessions of a Young Man" is the

first memoir of his dead life. From that crude beginning have come the lover of Doris and the companion of Stella during those Irish nights at Mount Venus, which were not the least of the scandal of "Hail and Farewell." The name of that hill outside Dublin was too authentic and appropriate to be ignored by an imaginative autobiographer in the final reincarnation of his dead self. Just as the theme of "Euphorion in Texas" could not fail to provoke an excellent tale in the manner of Boccaccio, though credible witnesses assert that on the night when Mr. Moore's visitor from Austin, Texas, was supposed to have called on her strange mission, no lady entered that now famous eighteenth-century house in Ely Place, Dublin, except a certain prominent Irish author of mature years, whose age and respectability placed her beyond the scope of the experiment related in that story of maternity for Art's sake.

It has been my amused good fortune to hear the ostensibly shameless author of "A Storyteller's Holiday" hesitate and apologize before daring to mention in the presence of a very modern young Frenchwoman the relatively harmless term *putain*. This affecting exhibition of early Victorian (or Second Empire) gallantry towards the once sheltered *jeune fille* is typical, it seems to me, of the contrast between the legendary George Moore of verbal ruthlessness and the real man. His delight in the interplay of sex is that of the artist. To dismiss his love stories or to accept them by the crude test of reality is to ignore the supreme function of sex in art. Remy de Gourmont's remarkable *Lettres à l'Amazone* lose none of their literary and psychological value because of the essentially intellectual quality of the romance which lay behind them.

George Moore's own theory concerning the transmutation of love affairs into literature was formulated definitely, for the first time, I think, in the following circumstances. In the summer of 1914 he wrote to me in Baltimore asking whether I could discover any trace of a girl about whom he has since written that "a garter and a lace handkerchief were treasured by me for many years, and the three letters she wrote to me; but in those days no order was kept among my papers; so nothing remains of her but a name, a name which she may have changed. Curious, isn't it, that I should remember her address through all these years? 17, Cathedral Street, Baltimore. . . . I might have married her, and if I had married her my life would have been quite different. I might have gone into business."

My mission was unsuccessful, for I had to report that there was no such number in Cathedral Street, and a prolonged search amongst the archives for the years in the 'Seventies, when the adventure of Marie Bruguère occurred, failed to reveal any evidence of her existence. H. L. Mencken became interested in the search for this fragment of Mr. Moore's dead life, but pronounced the affair to be "probably wholly imaginary." Whereupon I received this protest: "It may be that I have forgotten the number. I shouldn't like to think that this has happened, but even so my sin does not seem unforgivable, for have I not remembered her name, and the town and street she lived in for five-and-thirty years? Are there as many faithful hearts in your Baltimore?" Then came this declaration of principle. "It seems to me that an amatory indiscretion is only possible within a zone of ten or fifteen years; after five-and-twenty, love adventures are no longer indiscretions but matter for literary history."

Mr. Moore is not disposed to admit that his early works are even more obviously matter for literary history. He has so resolutely refused to consider them that Mr. St. John Ervine has rashly declared that he did not believe any one had ever seen or read those youthful poems, "Flowers of Passion" and "Pagan Poems," now the cherished possessions of the bibliophile. Although the author shudders at the mere sight of them, the books most emphatically exist as evidence of what a young man will write in Paris when lolling upon a couch "with royal fringes," and conscious of "the ideality" of his Japanese dressing-gown. With a profusion of gilt edges and a laureled skull and cross-bones, surmounted by a broken lyre, "Flowers of Passion" shrieks decadence from its very covers. The dedication is to an anonymous lady:

> Lean meward, O beloved! let me crown
> Thy brows with chaplet. Votive wreath I twine
> Of symbol flowers, and therein weave for sign,
>   From graft of passion, roses that have grown
> Bitter as frothing of blood. . . .

The volume then opens with an "Ode to a Dead Body" in the Baudelairian manner, which contains such beauties as

> Ay, verily, thou art a piteous thing,
> So awful is death's sting.
> Poor shameful lips! that never knew a kiss
> Of innocence, I wiss.

Then follow the inevitable "Laus Veneris" and
much talk of "odorous beds," "sweet breasts,"
strange sins, and swooning desires. Here in the
year of grace 1878, is all the stock-in-trade of the
Eighteen-nineties, merely awaiting the arrival of
similarly *fin de siècle* young men, but with some
power of writing good verse. It all looks in retrospect about as dangerous as that movie-vamp in-
terior in "Confessions of a Young Man." Yet
British virtue was outraged and a representative
critic declared that "this is a book that ought to
be burnt by the common hangman and its author
whipped at the cart's tail."

Its successor, "Pagan Poems," has no external
incitements to curiosity, being a conventional volume bound in black cloth, after the fashion of so
many books of verse of the period. It was, however, disowned by the publisher, who withdrew the
title-page, leaving the author free, however, to dis-
tribute these mutilated copies. Thus, in the one
which I possess, although the title-page is missing,
there is an inscription from the author to a lady
friend, showing that he was undeterred by the
wrath and scorn of the publisher. He even took
the trouble of revising some of the more defective
lines by writing in others. Again there is a dedication to a woman, this time in French, in which
his *"maîtresse des maîtresses"* is offered these poems
à défaut des caresses whose absence leaves him full
of *tristesses*. Several pieces are reprinted from the
earlier book, "Ballad of a Lost Soul, Sonnet,"
"The Corpse," "Bernice" and others. There are
slight verbal changes, such as the substitution of
"sorrowful" for "dernful," so that these poems may

be regarded as having satisfied the author as being
worth preserving. It would, nevertheless, be more
than indiscreet to quote them. In "A Love Letter,"
addressed to the Iza of the dedication, there recurs
the refrain:

> But well we knew, alas! my own sweet lady,
> That never have the stars of love shone steady.

If the constant repetition of such lines as those did
not mark their author as utterly without feeling for
the music of words, there still remains a mass of
dreadful evidence to that effect. One of the
poems, specially re-written for the recipient of the
book before me, contains this:

> A soldier burnt the temple of Ephesus,—
> It was, perhaps, a very dreadful deed,—
> But it preserved his name, Erostratus.

The second line is crossed out and the author's substitute was:

> It may have been but a barbaric deed.

In the circumstances it is not surprising that the
literary indiscretions of George Moore have been
more carefully concealed than his amatory indiscretions, though both may be the legitimate matter of
literary history. The only book of his nonage of
which Mr. Moore has spoken with his accustomed
candour is "Martin Luther: A Tragedy," which
appeared one year after "Flowers of Passion." It
was written in collaboration with Bernard Lopez,
who is described in "Confessions of a Young Man"
as one of the weird company which assembled at

the dinner table in the hotel of the youthful George Moore. "The little fat, neckless man, with the great bald head, fringed below the ears with hair, is Duval. He is a dramatic author—the author of one hundred and sixty plays. He does not intrude himself on your notice, but when you speak to him on literary matters he fixes a pair of tiny, sloe-like eyes on you, and talks affably of his collaborateurs."

This forgotten genius seems to have been a professional collaborator, and on the title-page of the five-act tragedy of "Martin Luther" his name is followed by the imposing list of those with whom Mr. Moore's collaborator had collaborated. The names are set out in the form of a pyramid: Scribe, Théophile Gautier, Dumas *père*, Gérard de Nerval, and eighteen obscurer talents. Clearly a startling send-off for the dramatic tyro, introduced as "George Moore, Author of 'Flowers of Passion'!" After each of them has dedicated the book, in French verse, to Swinburne, the correspondence of the collaborators is printed by way of a preface, because, as Moore says, "it is impossible to send our child naked into the world; we must write a preface; decency has always demanded a fig leaf, even of the Greek sculptors."

These eighteen letters may be cited as the authentic precursor of the prefaces subsequently made famous by Bernard Shaw. They are an amusing dissertation upon the art of playwriting in general and on "Martin Luther" in particular, with two interludes, consisting of a dramatization of an incident which occurred during Moore's journey to London from Paris, and a dream in five cantos about the decadence of the English stage.

Those frivolous preliminaries, however, hardly prepare the reader for the play itself, which is essentially the sort of blank verse tragedy that every young poet writes. It is the one work of his youth about which Mr. Moore could ever be induced to speak, when he saw those works of his age of innocence upon my bookshelf. He insists that it should be compared with his first novel, "A Modern Lover," for, as he said, "it appears that I could write verse at the age of three- or four-and-twenty much better than prose; there is a great deal of fustian in this drama, but the fustian seems to me to be well versified. . . . Everybody tries to write a blank verse drama when he is three-and-twenty, but he generally stops, possibly because he has less power. I bungled on to the end, translating Luther's celebrated hymn and making as good a translation as exists of it." George Moore's theological views have been copiously recorded in "Hail and Farewell"; he has given us his impressions "On Reading the Bible for the First Time"; in "The Brook Kerith" he has told the story of Christ. As a hymnologist he is not so well known, so I will quote indiscreetly the first verse of his rendering of Luther's hymn as an unexpected relic of his dead life:

> Our God, a right fast tower is He,
>   A sword and shield unshaken;
> From every need he helps us free,
>   That hath us overtaken.
> The old and evil foe
> Has come to work our woe—
> Much craft and greatest might
> His mail are for the fight:
> On earth is not his fellow.

27. WILLIAM BUTLER YEATS

THE Mechanics' Institute, in Abbey Street, Dublin, once the scene of the roughest vaudeville shows, in a town that at one time was less refined than it has since become. It is now the Abbey Theatre and the recently founded Irish National Theatre Society is beginning to enjoy the charm of an organized existence in a theater of its own. The audiences in the pit grow larger, but the orchestra stalls have that air of being a family affair which persisted until the heyday of the Irish dramatic revival had begun to appear as a memory. Only a few of those expensive seats were occupied and then, usually, by the initiated: Æ., George Moore, Edward Martyn, John Eglinton and the rest, but always and ever by W. B. Yeats and Lady Gregory. While she sat enthroned, already a species of dramatic dowager, W. B. Yeats flitted restlessly back and forth from back stage to stalls.

At the left-hand side of the stage, as the audience faced it, stood a curious little stairway of half a dozen steps, leading to a door which gave access to the rear of the house. With the invariability of clockwork, that little door would open, and down the steps would meditatively walk a tall, stooping figure, with pale face, pince-nez, flowing black tie and a great dark lock of hair which tumbled every moment over the left eye, and was mechanically brushed back with a rounded gesture of the most poetic hand. The figure would glide across the first row of the stalls and subside into a seat beside Lady Gregory. This ritual was a certain sign to the habitués that the curtain was about to rise, for the flitting figure was that of W. B. Yeats, whose comings and goings up and down those little stairs punctuated every act and bore witness to the period of the poet's most active interest in the affairs of the theater, an interest which was to have an opportunity a couple of years later of taking a stand which destroyed forever mob rule in the Irish Theatre.

Not quite so meditatively were those stairs ascended on the night in January, 1907, when the shifts of Synge's peasant girls were as red rags to the bulls which swore and hissed and booed and yelled and stamped their feet, in an effort to frighten Synge's "Playboy of the Western World" from the stage which it was to make world famous. Then around the walls of pit and stalls ranks of policemen stood, with orders to deposit in the street any person whose disapproval of Synge threatened to overcome the usual restraints of civilized people. And for one whole week that scene was repeated, until the play could be heard in perfect comfort, a week when those orchestra stalls lost all of their usual calm, and the flittings and consultations of the poet and Lady Gregory took on a significance where they had previously been more spectacular than anything else, spectacular to a point which prompted George Moore to a protest duly recorded in "Hail and Farewell."

To the eyes of youth the spectacle contained nothing of the sinister or ridiculous import upon which George Moore, it seems, insisted. With his verses in our ears, we were able, at the modest cost of one shilling, to contemplate the poet of our veneration at our leisure, to note every toss. of that rebellious lock, to watch at close quarters the contemplative figure whose passage relieved the streets of their peculiar Dublin drabness, which. is not without a charm of its own. While we assisted at the making of Irish literary history, we also had the good fortune to see, at the age when such things matter, a great poet who actually looked everything that a poet should be. It was not, I think, an illusion of youth that W. B. Yeats is the only writer in the English language in our time who not only did not look ridiculous in flowing tie, long hair and jacket of somber black or even velvet, but looked more properly attired than in the conventional garments of later years.

LONDON

An old-fashioned courtyard, given over to that mixture of private residence and petty trade which is the fate of such by-ways in London. One entered a diminutive hall and at once clambered up a precipitous staircase, leading into a somber, low-ceilinged room, full of books and pictures. A couple of bottles of wine and some glasses on the side-table, and round the hearth a circle, Arthur Rackham, Sturge Moore, repressed and taciturn, Ezra Pound, loquacious and aggressive in the declaration of old prejudices and new enthusiasms.

On a low seat in the corner, the master of this little house, W. B. Yeats, externally somewhat more of a personage, in the commonplace sense of the term, and not so impenitently and romantically the poet of other days. These are his English friends and disciples, and one looks in vain for that atmosphere of easy appreciation and deep respect, hidden under the appearance of casual friendliness, which marks his presence in such groups in Dublin. Here he says little, but is oracular. Some one declares, in the presence of this greatest and most authentic of Irish poets, that the Irish literary renaissance has produced nothing of any account, and his own work, between "The Wanderings of Oisin" and "The Wind Amongst the Reeds," is dismissed as youthful folly. The monstrous generalization fits so well into the self-critical mood of the poet's maturity that he makes no protest as concerns his own writings, although this blasphemy is intolerable to Irish ears from any lips but those of the singer of "Inisfree," of "The Hosting of the Sidhe" himself.

Here he seems to be a *déraciné*, and only those elements of his being and his poetry that are intellectual have validity. The gathering is formal and lacks the ease which belongs to deep associations and emotional bonds. The scene contrasts with that of an evening in Dublin in the old Queen Anne house of Oliver Gogarty, with windows looking onto the garden once the leased demesne of George Moore and celebrated by him. Æ. is there and these two life-long friends, with the stimulating seriousness and wit of their host to give edge to the conversation, talk of gods and heroes, of visions

and beliefs, and running through it all is the thread
of common culture, hopes and dreams. It contrasts,
too, with that other drawing-room of a queen-like
woman, now old and gray, with suffering as much
as with years, who once towered in the streets by
Yeats's side, moving with the grace of a swan, her
flaming gold hair the aureole of loveliness and
courage. Into that room Yeats would come, and
while heads were just turned to nod to him, he
would sink into a chair by the fire, lost in such
reveries as those later verses reveal—"Was there
another Troy for her to burn?" With the creator
of his Kathleen ni Houlihan before him, still passionate in her quest for freedom, he brooded:

FALLEN MAJESTY

Although crowds gathered once if she but showed her face,
And even old men's eyes grew dim, this hand alone,
Like some last courtier at a gypsy camping place
Babbling of fallen majesty, records what's gone.

The lineaments, a heart that laughter has made sweet,
These, these remain, but I record what's gone. A crowd
Will gather, and not know it walks the very street
Whereon a thing once walked that seemed a burning cloud.

WASHINGTON

Tea in the fashionable alley of the New Willard
Hotel, while throngs pass, paying no attention to a
tall, well-groomed gentleman, with rimless eye-
glasses, neat business suit, and starched collar.
The struggling of an embryonic lock would reveal
to closer scrutiny that the Irish poet, William But-

ler Yeats, is in town on his American lecture tour. Talk of Dublin, of old friends, of things past and accomplished, of the complications of that history of mine relating those achievements, of which he said, when the time came to pass judgment: "You refrained from an exceptional opportunity to be malicious." Yeats at his most human, animated and charming, achieving that superb comment upon George Moore, which I have recorded elsewhere in these impressions. It was inevitable that, contrary to the dictates of common sense, one should decide to hear the lecture, remembering those graceful addresses of old, when the needs of the Irish Theatre, the theories of Gordon Craig, the gospel of Tagore, were urged upon Dublin audiences in the most superb of artificial, studied but perfected public speeches.

A small hall crowded with hero-worshipers, for the most part Irish-Americans. The subject is a more or less wandering talk about the Irish Theatre, Irish literature and Yeats's own work in particular. In that peculiar, lilting, throaty enunciation of his, we heard for the first time a new poem which has since acquired a tragic significance, in the light of events that were to happen three years later:

> Was it for this the wild geese spread
> The gray wing upon every tide;
> For this that all the blood was shed,
> For this Edward Fitzgerald died,
> And Robert Emmet and Wolfe Tone,
> All that delirium of the brave?
> Romantic Ireland's dead and gone,
> It's with O'Leary in the grave.

Yet could we turn the years again,
And call those exiles as they were
In their loneliness and pain,
You'd cry "Some woman's yellow hair
Has maddened every mother's son";
They weighed so lightly what they gave,
But let them be, they're dead and gone,
They're with O'Leary in the grave.

The lecturer sat down to the accompaniment of much applause, and it soon became apparent, to any one who knew him, that he was in the process of abstracting himself as far as possible from the scene. A group of husky young women had prepared, as a special treat, that lovely song of his, "Down by the Sally Gardens," which they sang lustily, fortunately unaware that the author is tone-deaf. When they had finished, and the formal proceedings had closed, the crowd of hero-worshipers swarmed the platform. With democratic eagerness, strangers flung an arm around the poet's shoulder and called him brother. He, whose aloofness from the simplest human demonstrations of emotion is notorious, submitted apparently without an effort. He signed innumerable autographs, another practice of which he is ordinarily chary. I was once more plunged into amused admiration at the marvelous adaptability of literary visitors, once they come face to face with the ease and opportunity of America. I had seen others! But when saying good-by to him, I discovered the secret. He looked at me with unseeing eyes, and his hand mechanically took mine; by reflex action he murmured appropriate words. He had taken flight from his ignominy in a species of trance, leaving the shell of himself to pay the penalty of greatness.

DUBLIN

Now we have Senator Dr. William Butler Yeats, landed proprietor of a moated castle in Sligo, and the most conscientious legislator of the Irish Free State. The last phase of an amazing career, consecrated on its literary side by the award of the Nobel Prize. I like to remember what seem to me the first stages of this final incarnation. The poet and his wife are living in the village of Dundrum in the neighborhood of Dublin. They are temporarily installed in a hideous, square, Early-Victorian house, which has more the air of a camping-place than a home. In a room, cluttered with all the objects which lie about when one is not amongst one's own furniture and without accustomed facilities, we sat and talked, while a cat roamed about, showing all the signs of an uneasy conscience, as to which there was other more tangible evidence.

The mother and baby child were absent, and we talked of the then newly acquired castle in which he might never settle, for it was the most disturbed period of the Black-and-Tan régime. So little did he foresee his present rôle in the Irish Senate that his talk was of returning to Oxford and living in peace until such time as he could come over for the occasional enjoyment of the castle. He had just published that finest of his later works, "The Wild Swans at Coole," to which the title of its predecessor "Responsibilities" would so aptly have applied, for that was his mood, as his thoughts were resolutely turned upon his child, upon the new function of fatherhood so recently bestowed upon him. It was recounted, with something of Dublin's malicious glee, that when Yeats wrote his sonnet upon the Sinn Feiners executed in 1916, the poem was not completed until months after the event. On this occasion he had not been so slow. With a certain shy pride and diffidence unusual in him, he asked if I would like to hear some lines he had written for his little daughter.

In that nondescript furnished room, amid the distracting rustling of the cat's perambulations, I heard him intone, with an intensity of emotion characteristically at variance with the elaborate formality of the verses, which he read carefully from the manuscript in his small difficult writing:

A PRAYER FOR MY DAUGHTER

Once more the storm is howling and half hid
Under this cradle-hood and coverlid
My child sleeps on. There is no obstacle
But Gregory's wood and one bare hill
Whereby the haystack and roof-levelling wind,
Bred on the Atlantic, can be stayed;
And for an hour I have walked and prayed
Because of the great gloom that is in my mind.

I have walked and prayed for this young child an hour
And heard the sea-wind scream upon the tower,
And under the arches of the bridge, and scream
In the elms above the flooded stream;
Imagining in excited reverie
That the future years had come,
Dancing to a frenzied drum,
Out of the murderous innocence of the sea.

May she be granted beauty and yet not
Beauty to make a stranger's eye distraught,
Or hers before a looking-glass, for such,
Being made beautiful overmuch,

Consider beauty a sufficient end,
Lose natural kindness and maybe
The heart-revealing intimacy
That chooses right and never find a friend.

In courtesy I'd have her chiefly learned;
Hearts are not had as a gift but hearts are earned
By those that are not entirely beautiful;
Yet many, that have played the fool
For beauty's very self, has charm made wise,
And many a poor man that has roved,
Loved and thought himself beloved,
From a glad kindness cannot take his eyes.

And may her bride-groom bring her to a house
Where all's accustomed, ceremonious;
For arrogance and hatred are the wares
Peddled in the thoroughfares.
How but in custom and in ceremony
Are innocence and beauty born?
Ceremony's a name for the rich horn,
And custom for the spreading laurel tree.

28. JAMES STEPHENS

MY oldest and most enduring impression of
James Stephens is one of prodigious growth
from small beginnings. He is like one of
those genii in the "Arabian Nights" who rose out
of a small phial, until they revealed themselves in
their true and imposing proportions. Physically
he is a small, gnome-like creature; a powerful, tiny
elf, with a head whose shape is beautiful, and the
loveliest brown eyes, full of laughter, irreverence
and affection, set beneath a high sloping forehead
from which his black, curly hair has receded a little.
When I first met this tiny great man, he lived in a
tiny house and had published a tiny brown book
of verse, dedicated "To Æ. These," of which there
was much talk, soon diverted, however, to the three
books which in one full year were to make him
famous, "The Charwoman's Daughter," "The Hill
of Vision" and that "Crock of Gold" whose finest
passages were singled out for special praise by the
very people who had returned them unread when
they were submitted in the manuscript of an unknown author.

I remember the six stenographic notebooks in
which he had written with indelible pencil the rough
draft of "The Crock of Gold," before the work of
ceaseless revision at the huge typewriter which he
worked himself. When these three books were published, and those worn notebooks had served their
purpose and were despatched to the library of John

Quinn in New York, James Stephens celebrated his permanent liberty from the recently abandoned drudgery of a solicitor's office, and his momentary freedom from financial care, by the great hegira of his life, which has left a mark upon his career ever since. That tiny house was more crowded than it invariably and necessarily seemed, on the night when old friends and new admirers met to say good-by to Stephens before he left for one year's exile in Paris. With a feeling that something irreparable had happened, we saw him tear up his roots, and set out with wife and children, two cats of royal breed, and all his illusions, to sit about in cafés, talk to American newspapermen, and write such stories as made up his next and feeblest book, "Here Are Ladies."

On his return, the cats were as proud and shy as ever, the children more remarkably like leprechauns, in their little green jersey suits and green peaked caps, while his wife had tasted of such mythical joys as the tradition of Paris has imposed upon her sex. James Stephens himself had acquired a blue French *pélerine*, which enveloped him in a way that added greatly to the elfin quality of his appearance. He had engaged in a hand-to-hand fight with the French language, and recounted with glee an incident of the encounter when, on ordering *un vin blanc gommé*, he was presented ceremoniously with a postage stamp reposing in the chilly center of a large plate. He also brought back a taste for French bread which he gratified to the extent of marching homewards every evening with a lengthy crisp roll under his arm, to the astonishment of the untraveled, unused to such a sight in the streets of any town, much less in those of their familiar Dublin. He had retained his flat near the Boulevard Montparnasse, and almost every year since, he has returned to satisfy his curious craving for life in its sheer externals, as viewed from an endless succession of café tables, at which he can never sit often enough or too long.

He was appointed Assistant to the Director of the National Gallery of Ireland, and evolved into the most engaging Civil Servant imaginable. His offices, above the Gallery, were lighted by two dignified *œils-de bœuf*, and furnished like the library of a wealthy connoisseur. The position and the place seemed designed by Providence to give an artist security and leisure. Up that spiral staircase of highly polished sandstone few care to come disturbing his infinite leisure, and one lion-hunter was rewarded for her importunity by falling down and breaking her leg—although with a sense of humor, which Stephens appreciated, she declared that he had thrown her down. When coal was expensive and unprocurable, during the war, it was pleasant to sit before a piled-up, roaring fire, in a comfortable armchair, and disperse the *ennui* of this exemplary official, who was always at his post, but could never, he declared, do any work of his own during the secluded hours of his subsidized leisure. The very purpose for which kind destiny arranges such employments was defeated.

However, it was possible to talk there, for it is inconceivable that there is any place or circumstance where the enchanting flow, or more accurately, the scintillating skip, of James Stephens's conversation would cease. I believe he actually developed the technique of personally conducting highly recommended and distinguished visitors around the Gallery, and would affix his monocle and make remarks appropriate to the occasion. Only once did I allow him to don the eyeglass of his office in my honor, and that was when he took me to look at Sargent's symbolical picture of Woodrow Wilson, which the Directors, mistaking patriotic enthusiasm for artistic discrimination, had acquired at great expense. Usually the hours spent in the Gallery were devoted to literature. There Stephens confessed his raptures when he discovered vast quantities of the "Top Notch Magazine" in an outpost of American civilization, to wit, the Dublin branch of the Woolworth stores. For this red-blooded fiction he had an enthusiasm which I could never induce him to give to "Jurgen," although I presented him with the valuable first edition of that work—unaware, I confess, of its worth in the eyes of collectors—which he passed on unread to Æ. As a critic James Stephens startles one by the incongruity of his enthusiasms rather than by the soundness of his judgments. For W. B. Yeats, Æ. and George Moore he has an admiration which he does not bestow on any other of his Irish contemporaries. James Joyce he finds as unreadable as, I suspect, his own works are to Joyce. He has a conviction, which he utters half-whimsically, half-seriously, that he himself is the greatest living prose writer. There are times when his assertion must strike even the most critical. There are none when his claim seems utterly without foundation.

James Stephens is a writer whose real gift is that of the Irish *shanachie;* he is a born story-teller.

When he reads his work, he never fails to bring out
every fine quality in his writing, and now and then,
his skill is such that he quite unconsciously conceals
defects. It seemed to me when I heard him read
the poems in "Green Branches," inspired by the
loss of his friends in the Insurrection of 1916, that
he had never done anything more beautiful, and
the emotion in his voice was also in the moving
words:

> Be green upon their graves, O happy Spring,
> For they were young and eager who are dead;
> Of all things that are young and quivering
> With eager life be they remembered:
> They move not here, they have gone to the clay,
> They cannot die again for liberty;
> Be they remembered of their land for aye;
> Green be their graves and green their memory.
>
> Fragrance and beauty come in with the green,
> The ragged bushes put on sweet attire,
> The birds forget how chill these airs have been,
> The clouds bloom out again and live in fire;
> Blue is the dawn of day, calm is the lake,
> And merry sounds are fitful in the thorn;
> In covert deep the young black birds awake,
> They shake their wings and sing upon the morn.
>
> At springtime of the year you came and swung
> Green flags above the newly-greening earth;
> Scarce were the leaves unfolded, they were young,
> Nor had outgrown the wrinkles of their birth:
> Comrades they thought you of their pleasant hour,
> They had but glimpsed the sun when they saw you;
> They heard your songs e'er birds had singing power,
> And drank your blood e'er that they drank the dew.

When he was writing the volume of "Irish Fairy
Tales" and his more recent "Deirdre," he read

every chapter to a circle of a few friends, one an expert Irish scholar, upon whom he relied for historical accuracy in his re-molding of the legendary Gaelic material. "Deirdre" was the first of five volumes in which he planned to re-tell the great epic cycle as it had never been done before, to infuse into the characters his own imagination and fancy, to endow his country with what he promised would be an Irish "Arabian Nights." Parts of the first book entranced us, as he read them, perched on a chair in his characteristic attitude, his feet resting on a rung and his body inclined forward. But afterwards, on comparing impressions with Æ. and others who were present, I found that all agreed that many weaknesses had escaped as we listened, which were evident in the printed book. There were scenes, such as the escape of Deirdre in the moonlight and her meeting with Naisi, which are equal to the best in "The Demi-Gods" and "The Crock of Gold," but in several places the boisterous, grotesque humor of the author had carried him away.

The writing of this epic has been, however, an antidote to the process of denationalization which has threatened Stephens ever since his first residence in France. For one thing, it set him seriously to work on the Irish language, for without Irish he could not reach the sources of his inspiration. From this language he derived more pleasure and more advantage than from French, and his combined philological and literary enthusiasm were a pleasant spectacle. He attended classes and, at the same time buried himself in the learned publications containing the old Irish texts. His chief companion

in this always exciting enterprise,—to an Irishman,
—of learning his more or less native tongue, was his
friend Stephen MacKenna, Gaelic scholar, Hel-
lenist and collector of folk-music.

MacKenna had only one practical problem, to
disentangle his name from that of the popular novelist, Stephen McKenna, which he did by modest
insistence on the philological accuracy of his own
Mac. Otherwise, he divided his time between his
great translation of Plotinus and the playing of
Irish folk-music on the concertina, with Irish conversation whenever any one could be found who
simultaneously knew Irish and was worth talking
to—a difficult combination in a town where all the
best talk is in English. In James Stephens he found
an ideal ally, for both are brilliant talkers, and so
entirely dissimilar that their common interest in
slender vowels and other marvels of the Irish language enhanced the contrasted pleasure of their
company. Stephen MacKenna is the best surviv-
ing example of that type of intensely Irish, yet cosmopolitan Irishmen, who carried their sword, their
Catholicism and their personal charm to France and
Spain in the seventeenth century. He is the lineal
descendant of the Wild Geese. In his youth he had
gone off to Greece to fight the Turks; he had lived
many years in Paris, and spoke French and Irish
as fluently as English. A born philologist, and a
monk of learning truly medieval, he lived only for
his Plotinus, his music and his Irish, and the first
two handsome quarto volumes of his translation of
the Enneads, the only scholarly English version
that is also literature, are monuments to his patience
in carrying out a great task under inconceivable

difficulties of ill-health. These two men would sit in MacKenna's library, strewn with music, the beloved concertina reposing on the piano, and the bookcases filled with the strangest collection of books. A whole set of Huysmans, all inscribed affectionately by the author, a great hoard of books in the Irish language, and a special collection of Neo-Platonic literature. It was an irony of fate that the Plotinus of Stephen MacKenna should be issued in the luxurious quartos of the Medici Society, for he displayed his contempt for rare editions and books as books in a most original manner. He would break volumes in half for convenient reading, and even tear out all the pages of a book except those which he actually needed. The juxtaposition of "Seumas" and "Stiofan" was one of the happiest of Nature's devices for proving that all is—sometimes—right with the world. When Æ. supervened, and MacKenna pitted his sincere Catholic mysticism against the teaching of Buddha, with Stephens hovering about them, metaphorically, like a gently malicious sprite, the spectacle was vastly entertaining.

The malicious humor of James Stephens often takes a sharper form, especially when he is threatened by bores. When the author of "Set Down in Malice" arrived in Dublin to show up the people whom he did not know, as he had already shown up his friends in England, the inevitable but tacit agreement was reached to set this English journalist as far wrong as possible. Astonishing feats of ignorance and insolence were performed for his benefit, some of which are recorded by the innocent victim in the sequel, "Set Down in Friendship." When

Gerald Cumberland called on James Stephens, he mentioned H. G. Wells. Whereupon Stephens, adjusting his monocle, inquired gravely: "Wells? Who is Wells? Is he dead? Does he write?" Whence Mr. Cumberland was moved to the loftiest pity for the provincial ignorance and self-sufficiency of the Irish intellectuals.

Kindness and good humor, however, are the essence of James Stephens. The whole man is in his writings, from the impish irreverence of "Insurrections" to the haunting pathos of "Reincarnations," with all the expanse of child-like fancy in "The Charwoman's Daughter" and the grotesque laughter of "The Crock of Gold" between. Pity and suffering, too, have gone into the making of him, and have sharpened that uncanny faculty of his, which enables him to establish himself on the friendliest terms with dumb animals, whose thoughts he can record with a whimsical tenderness. His soft brown eyes are lit at once by the highest intelligence and by that profound, inarticulate love, which one never sees unmoved in the eyes of the finer animals. This gnome, this elfin wit, the James Stephens of quips and fancies that bubble into laughter, of sensitive emotions that soar into prose and poetry of freshest beauty, is the James Stephens, above all, who has a fine soul.

29. GEORGE W. RUSSELL (Æ.)

THE essentially dignified editorial sanctum of of the Unionist "Irish Times," that prosperous home of lost causes, is not exactly the place where one would expect to begin a friendship with a man whose genius is the embodiment of all the elements, political, intellectual and artistic, which spelled the doom of Unionist Ireland. It was there, however, that I first met Æ.

A certain number of—more or less literary—heretics used to occupy the chair of Assistant Editor, it being understood that their editorial homilies would be restricted to matters of relative unimportance, which amounted, in practice, to every aspect of human endeavor and folly except the sacrosanct theme of Ireland's unalterable devotion to the Union with England. Whenever this question was involved, directly or indirectly—which is to say, every day—only the hallowed and consecrated pen of the Editor himself could be entrusted with the leading article concerned. Thus, one sat nightly elaborating discourses on such inconsequential subjects as the Italian war in Tripoli, Post-Impressionist Painting, the latest discoveries in science, the most recent outrage of militant feminism. In the adjoining room the carefully modulated tones of the Editor could be heard as he dictated—for his pen was a metaphor—the first leader of the day. With perfect precision his dictation fell into the three traditional paragraph lengths which made the requisite column. The mathematical exactness of this operation was as perfectly mechanical as the sentiments expressed. One could almost hear the click of each paragraph, when the speaker paused, as it dovetailed into its neighbor.

About midnight a huge cup of very strong tea was served, and it was usually after being fortified by this indispensable Irish stimulant that one devoted the last hour, until 1 A.M. to the elucubration of articles which would create the illusion that the "Irish Times" was interested in other things besides the menace of Home Rule—as we then described the modest ambitions of Parnell and John Redmond. It was a few moments before this frenzied and desperate activity, when a tall figure, with curly brown beard and ruffled hair, entered my room in the company of a friend, who introduced me to George Russell. I shook a hand, small and soft and beautifully shaped, which has never known the artificial aids with which so many vainly try to achieve that natural beauty. The name and all it stood for were, of course, long familiar to me, and I at once brought a gleam of response into those fascinating gray-blue eyes, that seem so long and narrow and profound, when I challenged some favorite doctrine of his, fresh in my mind from a reading of a recent number of "The Irish Homestead." That fabulous "agricultural" paper has now evolved into a frankly literary and political weekly, under another name, but for many of the formative years of my generation, it combined instruction in all branches of farming with such a passion for literature and ideas that it was the center of culture at once universal and national.

This brief interchange of views concluded with an invitation to "write that to me in 'the Homestead,' " which I did with an ardor engendered, in my experience, only by the extraordinary maieutic quality of Æ.'s encouragement, that fertility and prodigality of ideas in the man, which has put into his debt every writer who has known him. As a combative opponent I was welcomed editorially, for his is not that order of greatness which responds only to agreement and flattery. In retrospect it seems to me that I *opposed* my way into his friendship, for the result of much written disagreement was a further invitation to come and see him whenever I wanted to talk. Sunday nights were set apart for such meetings, and soon, like so many dozens of visitors, important and trivial, transitory and regular, I found my way to Æ.'s. The door was unlatched, so that one could come in and join the circle without disturbing the conversation, a useless precaution, however, for he was always out in the hall welcoming his guest with outstretched hands before the latter had closed the door to again.

Two long rooms ran from the front of the house to the back, and here the people were gathered, first in the back room, and then overflowing into the front, if the evening were crowded. Around the room were pictures by Æ. and his friends, with many of his own compositions standing on easels or lined against the wall, for this was his studio during working hours. Two tables received the piled-up mass of books and periodicals, lying in the disorder of whatever chance placed them there in the course of months and years. In one corner stood bookshelves containing Æ.'s own works, and an epitome of the new Irish literature which had grown up with him, many rare inscribed volumes by authors delectable both to bibliophiles and readers. In another corner was his vast library of Oriental and occult literature, while two other sets of shelves contained the miscellaneous books accumulated by this omnivorous reader, who treasured a battered reprint of "The Three Musketeers" as carefully—and as carelessly!—as the privately printed presentation copy of Yeats's "Tables of the Law." I once attempted to put a librarian's order into this artist's chaos, and for weeks no book could be found by its owner, until gradually the original disorder was restored by the process which created it, and only the general landmarks I have described roughly indicated a course through this sea of print.

So long as there were seats for the visitors, they did not have to practice the art of sitting on the floor, in which Æ. is as much at home as an Indian mystic. It is doubtless part of that curious alliance of his whole being with Oriental mysticism, which has given a universal mind to a man who has never traveled beyond England and whose whole life has been spent in Ireland. His universality of outlook, his cosmic imagination and his deep attachment to his native land are the three qualities in Æ. to which may be traced the paradox of an existence that is alternately and simultaneously that of a poet, painter, economist and philosopher. To them also he owes the attraction which he exercises upon all sorts of diverse people. Mahatma Ghandi and Lloyd George, the secretary of a coöperative store and the bashful young author of an unpublished

epic, Rabindranath Tagore and James Larkin—all
such disparate personalities will—and in many cases
have—found in him a friend and a counselor.

Even James Joyce, hyper-sensitive and touchy,
did not always resist him, in spite of the deliberate
mockery which is the lot of Æ., as of other Dubliners, in "Ulysses." When Joyce was leaving Ireland he came to Æ. with a small packet, carefully
wrapped in oilskin tissue to preserve it from the
inclemencies of time. It was his one cherished possession, which he wished to place in safe-keeping so
that, if any accident befell him, as he explained, his
name would be immortalized. Æ. received the
packet with appropriate emotion, and was authorized, at the same time, to examine its contents, to
assure himself that it was no ordinary commission
with which he had been entrusted. He undid the
wrappers and found, carefully copied out on little
squares of paper, in Joyce's best handwriting, the
poems which afterwards achieved such immortality,
at least, as copyright could confer, by appearing in
London as "Chamber Music." There was then, as
Æ. declared, not enough chaos in James Joyce to
make a world. When he later wrestled with
"Ulysses" in the mangled, misprinted pages of
"The Little Review," he confessed to being baffled
by such chaos as none in Dublin at that time could
have foreseen, not even the author of "Dubliners"
himself, if his early writings are to be taken as an
indication.

He is the one man in Ireland so far above suspicion of self-seeking and personal vanity, so mani-
festly serene, generous, well-informed and detached,
impartial and responsive, that his relations with the

turbulent world in which he has worked so faith-
fully, with such single-minded devotion, are unique
in any country. To him came red-tabbed generals
of the British army of occupation and fugitives
from Black-and-Tan terrorism, Republicans with
minds closed to all reason, and cautious negotiators
in search of compromises, strike-leaders and champions of capitalism, young Irishmen in khaki home
from the Somme and their brothers, perhaps, in the
gray-green uniform of Sinn Fein, advocates of Parliamentary Home Rule and Dominion Home Rule,
of closer union with England and of separatism
such as can never be known on land or sea in this
modern world. In Æ. they have confided their
fears and problems, and he has not failed them.
In all the plans and hopes and dreams, the movements and enterprises which have transformed
Ireland in his lifetime Æ. has been concerned, or
indirectly involved. But his name will not be found
on any roll of official honors, nor in any spectacular
distribution of rewards for services, avowed or sur-
reptitious. His place is more dignified and secure;
his reward more enduring.

His public position is characteristic of his life and
personality. In this, as in all things, he is himself.
Otherwise, his relations with every camp might be
explicable by the cunning of the common oppor-
tunist. Whereas the virtue of Æ.'s unique situation is that never did a man more consistently and
resolutely declare and uphold his own convictions;
in a country, too, where stereotyped divisions and
mass action had come, by reason of historic circumstance, to be regarded as essential and desirable.
Yet, he did not lose the respect of any but those

who themselves did not deserve respect, the incurably inferior. When the young poet came down from his Ulster countryside to Dublin, his first compelling impulse was to proclaim in the realm of religious experience "the golden heresy of truth," an astounding gesture in the eyes of a people for whom religion had acquired the value of a class distinction and a political banner. Here was one who saw visions, but abhorred the cheap mystery-mongering of spook-hunters and table-turners, who painted pictures of the elemental Beings he had seen, and who discusses spiritual phenomena as if such psychic experiences were those of everyday life, yet dismisses the divagations of the professional mediums and their credulous dupes. Æ.'s mysticism bears about the same relation to that of the popular prophets of the mystic and occult as his politics do to the dreary tub-thumping and impudent humbug of professional politicians. To argue with him as one would with a Conan Doyle or an Oliver Lodge would be unintelligent. He is not a reporter of ectoplasmatic gymnastics or the celestial cigars and whiskies and sodas of "Raymond"; he is a mystic poet and teacher of the race of William Blake.

He has the modesty of the superior man, and never once in the circles which invariably form about him wherever he is have I seen him dogmatic, vain, or complacently brilliant. He listens with an intelligent eagerness which is all the more remarkable because there are a few sides of human activity and speculation upon which he has not reflected. His qualities, when enumerated abstractly, are misleading as to their effect upon his personality, for he lacks completely the pontifical assurance of the latter-day prophet, the affectations so strenuously cultivated by lesser men of his temperament. It is the human being in him that predominates, and all his attainments serve only to emphasize the high human quality in him, as they are bent on that emphasis in his exercise of his genius. He appeals at once to heart and brain, so that it is impossible to like him without admiring him, or to admire him without gratefully surrendering one's affection. John Eglinton defined the peculiar emotion he arouses as Ætheism, but the feeling which Æ. inspires is not that of a cult. In the prolonged hours which I have spent with him, my impenitent rationalism was always pitted against his mysticism, and amongst those close to him there has always been that independence in relation to his views and beliefs as he himself has maintained as against those of others. He is not the leader of an æsthetic chapel.

The literature which he has given us and the literature which he has inspired are equally independent of each other. James Stephens, I suppose, is the greatest of the many writers whom he discovered and fostered, and if the imprint of Æ.'s mind upon that irreverent, fantastic genius cannot be denied, his complete originality is even more obvious. Like all great teachers, Æ. has nothing in him of the pedant and the pedagogue, and his satisfaction is not in his echoes, but in the personalities which he has been the first to perceive and which he can help towards self-realization, the more complete the more it diverges from him. He believes that in the development of real individuality and character lies the only method of producing fine life and fine art. His fundamental religious faith in the divinity in man enables him to maintain an optimism denied to the cynical, and perhaps to discern the spark that is concealed—and on occasion to imagine one that is not there. He is without naïveté, but prefers to allow others to be cynical for him. His own method of revenge is a gentle but devastating wit, as when he recently traced the history of a notorious political charlatan as though the culprit were the imaginary hero of a strange, Irish Expressionist novel.

His wit and his intellectual range and fertility are the magnets that drew those interesting groups to his home on Sunday evenings. They are, of course, the secret and essence of good conversation, and Æ. is one of the finest conversationalists of his generation. I have heard the longest and most abstruse philosophical debates move on over the whole field of science and metaphysics into the small hours of the morning. Not a moment is dull, nor are there any arid patches of dry-as-dust learning, although authorities, experiments and researches are drawn upon at every turn of the discussion. For many nights I upheld against him the rationalistic ethics of Schopenhauer, while he retorted with his own interpretation of the Sacred Books of the East. As sheer intellectual exercises those talks remain with me amongst the best memories, yet he had no equipment in German philosophy and I had done little more than skim a translation from the Upanishads, made by his friend Charles Johnston in the early days of the theosophical movement in

Dublin. With Æ. minds meet in the play of words and ideas, without that preliminary agreement, or that mutual conning of identical documents, which are usually essential to what pompous mediocrities deem "serious conversation."

Solemn pedantry and solemn fooling have no part in Æ.'s scheme of things. In spite of a certain amount of formal education, he is one of the most educated men alive. His learning is considerable and what emerges from it is alive, varied, spontaneous and human, indelibly marked by his own personality. He has fewer accumulations of useless knowledge than any man whom I have known. It seems as if no word, no experience, has ever been wasted upon him, that everything has gone into the formation of his mind and character and become an integral part of it. No ostentatious accomplishment, no obtrusive acquisition, stands out to impress the unitiated. He is a harmoniously developed man, a complete individual, whose faith in individualism is so strong that his social scheme is a coöperative commonwealth of such individuals. His generosity is such that he can see around him every evidence of the actual quality of human nature, yet believe in its potentialities. That is why there is in him an immediate response to every manifestation of individuality, and a marked antipathy for crowds and their idols. That is why he can enjoy himself with his friend the Rabelaisian Polish painter, Casimir Markiewicz, as well as with the sardonic wit, Oliver Gogarty; why he appreciated the prose of James Stephens, the poetry of Seumas O'Sullivan and the plays of Padraic Colum; why he realized the brilliance of T. M. Kettle and the social significance of James Connolly. He attracts first-rate men and stirs what is best in all of us. His personality dominates every constructive phase of modern Irish thought, but he himself is selfless. In short, Æ. has in him all that one tries to sum up by saying: He is a great man.

THE END

DATE DUE

30 505 JOSTEN'S			